THE TRUTH ABOUT
ABOUT
HIRING THE BEST

Cathy Fyock

PEARSON
Prentice Hall
BUSINESS

Harlow, England • London • New York • Boston • San Francisco • Toronto
Sydney • Tokyo • Singapore • Hong Kong • Seoul • Taipei • New Delhi
Cape Town • Madrid • Mexico City • Amsterdam • Munich • Paris • Milan

PEARSON EDUCATION LIMITED

Edinburgh Gate
Harlow CM20 2JE
Tel: +44 (0)1279 623623
Fax: +44 (0)1279 431059
Website: www.pearsoned.co.uk

First published in Great Britain 2008

The right of Cathy Fyock to be identified as author of this work has been asserted by her in accordance with the Copyright, Designs and Patents Act 1988.

ISBN: 978-0-273-71533-7

British Library Cataloguing-in-Publication Data
A catalogue record for this book is available from the British Library

Original edition, entitled TRUTH ABOUT HIRING THE BEST, THE, 1st Edition, by FYOCK, CATHY, published by Pearson Education, Inc, publishing as FT PRESS, Copyright © 2008.

This edition published by PEARSON EDUCATION LTD, Copyright © 2008.

This edition is manufactured in Great Britain and is authorized for sale only in UK, EUROPE, MIDDLE EAST AND AFRICA.

10 9 8 7 6 5 4 3 2 1
11 10 09 08 07

Typeset in 10pt Meta Light LF by 3
Printed and bound in Great Britain by Ashford Colour Press Ltd, Gosport

The publisher's policy is to use paper manufactured from sustainable forests.

The day you're given the assignment to fill an open position is the day you're invited to change the world and leave a legacy that could outlast you for generations. There's a ripple effect with every hiring decision you make that goes beyond the simple transaction that begins with the question, "How soon can you start?" It's not unlike the realization that Jimmy Stewart's character, George Bailey, discovered in the classic movie *It's a Wonderful Life*: The life of an individual does matter and can make a big difference for his family, his friends, and his community. And the decision you make about who you will hire will have similar dramatic consequences for you, the person you hire, and the life of your organization.

This book is designed to help you focus on the all-important employment process, beginning with how you identify the best candidates for your team, to how you develop a pool of top candidates, to how you select the best person for the job. It is a comprehensive book focusing on all the issues that impact the quality of your team.

This book is based on my experiences as a staffing specialist, an HR generalist, a hiring manager, and a consultant specializing in recruiting, selecting, and retaining employees in an aging and changing workplace. For the first 10 years of my career, I worked as a human resources professional with a strong focus in staffing. Over the past 20 years I've helped organizations in many industries across the United States develop a strategic approach to staffing and employment.

Here's what I've learned: The practices that you may have been using for years might not be serving you well. Many hiring managers believe that they know how to recruit and select employees because they've been doing it for so long. Other managers believe that conventional wisdom can help in the process. This book is designed to challenge some of this conventional wisdom about staffing and offer you the truth, and nothing but the truth.

No future will be exactly the same based upon the choices that you make. Realize that making a choice of candidate A will lead to future A, and that a choice of candidate B will lead to future B. If you choose a candidate who is a risk taker, loves a challenge, and embraces change and innovation, your organization will likely foster a risk-taking, innovative culture. If you choose a candidate who is hungry for knowledge and is a life-long learner, your organization will likely foster a growth culture.

Maybe your inclination is to hire someone just like the last incumbent in the job. If that's the case, you may be choosing a future that is a lot like your past. Or, you might take a risk and hire someone who is unlike not only the last person in that role, but unlike you as well. You're more likely to be headed for a different and unique future.

Understand that the quality of your hiring decision will not only impact the future of the organization, it will likely impact your personal future as well. If you hire a strong performer with excellent skill sets—and who fits into the company's future plans—you'll not only make yourself look good by developing a strong team, you'll also be building a prosperous career for yourself.

So the choice is yours. And it's bigger than just this one task of filling a position.

TRUTH

1

There is no such thing as *the* ideal candidate

We all know what makes an ideal candidate. We all want employees with a great attitude, strong work ethic, high energy, and strong motivation. We also want employees who can work as part of a team, provide great customer service, and have passion about their work and loyalty to their employer. Right? Wrong!

There is no universally ideal candidate. In fact, we all have slightly different ideas about what makes a great employee.

At a hiring seminar, managers were asked to identify the traits of their ideal candidate, with wildly varying results. Some wanted an assistant who thought like they did; others wanted someone with skills opposite their own. Certain managers wanted their employees to have the ability to think independently; others wanted people who could follow the established practices and procedures prescribed by their organization. Some wanted assistants who would be bubbly and outgoing; others wanted introverts who could work on their own.

For example, in a company where employees must work together as a cohesive team, the quality of team orientation will be paramount in the job specifications. However, some organizations, such as home health agencies with employees who travel to the homes of frail, elderly, and sick clients, may need strong individual contributors who can work independently to solve problems while in the client's home. While many organizations, such as graphic design studios, value creativity and originality of thought, other organizations, like fast food restaurants and banks, may need food service workers or bank tellers to follow very specific guidelines and policies for doing their work.

Similarly, you may believe that going to "A" schools is the way to get "A" candidates. This isn't necessarily true. For example, when Kentucky Fried Chicken was recruiting for fast track managers, it found that some of the "best" schools' students weren't necessarily open to supervisory roles in fast food, although they had a great track record of promoting into top management those who began as food service associates or as supervisors. In fact, they discovered that when they attended some of the career

There is no universally ideal candidate.

fairs at the best hospitality management schools, students were not looking at fast food as their ultimate goal. They also discovered that one of the best colleges for recruitment efforts was at a local college that had many nontraditional students (older students with a strong work history). Recruitment success—from a B school!

As you outline the key candidate dimensions, make sure you also assess your culture to ensure there's a match between what you need from your employees and what you have to offer them in terms of consistency and culture. To get a handle on what your organizational and departmental culture is all about, think about "who we are," "what we do," and "how we do it." Check your answers with your colleagues to see if there is consistent agreement. You might also conduct a focus group with your team or strategize at a retreat or staff meeting. Your rank-and-file employees, front-line employees, and customers may see your organization differently. Your leaders may see the company as a service-driven organization, which may be true of your external positioning but may not be true in how the company actually responds to employee needs and concerns.

One organization identified its core values, sometimes called *organizational competencies*, by gathering groups of employees and supervisors to discuss what it was the organization valued in terms of behaviors. The groups were asked, "When you observe employees exhibiting the values of this organization, what do you see or hear them doing?" Through a series of focus groups and managerial discussions, this organization was able to create its list of the groups' organizational values, which were then used as a tool in employee selection and in performance management. This process allowed this business to not only select employees who were aligned with its values, but also to then reinforce the behaviors it wanted to see in its employees.

> To get a handle on what your organizational and departmental culture is all about, think about "who we are," "what we do," and "how we do it."

TRUTH

2

You are a seller in a buyer's market

You're feeling pretty good these days—maybe even a little bit smug. Job seekers are banging on your employment door, clamoring for the chance to work for you. "This is great," you think. "I don't have to go out and recruit since so many people obviously want to work for our organization. I can just cherry-pick the very best applicants."

Not so fast. The people who are clamoring to work for your team may not be the ones you want to hire. If they're desperate to work for you, that desperation may be because they're having trouble finding jobs with anyone else. People who are actively seeking employment are most likely to be unhappy with their current circumstances. Or they don't have a job at all. And there may be a very good reason why not. But don't be surprised to see their faces at your door.

It's far better to attract the folks who are loyal to their employers, have excellent work habits, get along with others, and love their work. Unfortunately, it's hard to find these individuals. With unemployment rates reaching record lows, most of today's most desirable employees are already employed someplace else. These passive job seekers might explore a job opportunity only if it is presented to them. In the meantime, they just aren't out there knocking on doors. They are happily focusing on their work, oblivious to your recruitment needs.

But you can still find and recruit these best employees. You just have to be purposeful about it. They're hanging out in the hidden candidate market and have better uses for their newspaper-reading or Web-prowling time than looking for a new job.

Here are some ways you can attract these elusive job seekers inexpensively and effectively:

> It's far better to attract the folks who are loyal to their employers, have excellent work habits, get along with others, and love their work.

- Use third-party recruiters to solicit high-quality candidates working for someone else. They usually require a hefty fee (around 30 percent of annualized base), but it may be worth it.

- Get on the phone and call people you know and trust: your customers, your peers in related companies, your vendors, even your competitors. They may make an excellent referral.

- Ask your employees to refer their friends and colleagues.

- Make friends with the career counselors at your local colleges and high schools. Let them know what kinds of employees you're on the lookout for, and let them do your scouting for you.

- Don't require a resume as the first step in the process. Remember that only active job seekers have prepared resumes.

- Make it easy for job candidates who are working elsewhere to come in and apply with you. Offer some options for evening or weekend appointments to attract happily employed candidates.

Keep in mind that you're a seller, and this is a buyer's market. Most candidates who are happily employed elsewhere will need to be "sold" on the idea of working for you. Therefore, you cannot merely list the job requirements (what you expect from them) in your print and online recruitment messages. You need to "woo" candidates by spelling out what advantages they can expect from you.

TRUTH

3

Catch the boomerangs

Susan left your department after receiving an irresistible offer from another company. She was a great employee, and you were sorry to see her go. But you also understood that this was an opportunity she just couldn't pass up.

Now she wants to come back. Should you consider rehiring her?

It used to be that employees, once having left the organization, would never consider returning. And employers would never consider hiring them back. A lot of ego, hurt feelings, and sense of betrayal were wrapped up in those resignations. Today, these returning employees—or "boomerangs"—could be your best employment bet.

If you need what Susan has to offer, roll out the red carpet!

Many organizations, starting with those in high-tech industries where the demand for qualified, experienced technology workers is high, welcome back those employees who left the company looking for that ideal job. Today, nearly 60 percent of midsize and large companies will rehire high-performing IT and business professionals to meet job demands and cut recruitment time and expense. And the use of returning employees is quickly expanding to other industries and fields, including retail and manufacturing.

These boomerang employees may be a valuable population for you to consider as you recruit. They already know your business and internal culture, so your on-boarding expenses and time could be cut significantly. They're coming back with additional skills and experience, thanks to their most recent employer, with valuable training and development that you didn't have to pay for. They may also help convince their fellow employees that your organization is worthy of their loyalty and commitment.

> Today, these returning employees— or "boomerangs"— could be your best employment bet.

If you are interested in hiring back boomerang employees with a strong work record, let the word get out that yours is the kind of company culture that appreciates all its employees, even the ones who have left, and then borrow ideas from colleges for ways of staying in touch with them.

Managers, in realizing that their "alums" are an important constituency, may want to keep the connection going. Having lunch or coffee or meeting for an after-hours drink with the old team may be an easy way to keep in touch with those who you'd love to have back. Keep the connection going by emailing your past team members on what's happening in the organization— new projects, promotions, and, of course, vacancies.

Other organizations re-recruit their former employees in even more assertive ways. For example, one hospital in Nebraska conducted exit interviews by phone with employees who had recently left the organization. If eligible for rehire and worthy of an invitation to return, the former employee was welcomed back to work. The program was successful in opening the door for these employees who thought the grass was greener elsewhere but discovered that it wasn't.

There are some issues that might complicate the re-employment of the returning boomerang:

- If she was working for a direct competitor, for instance, the boomerang may be bound by a noncompete agreement.

- Can you place the boomerang in a position that can appropriately use—and reward—the new levels of experience and expertise? Ideally, you'll be rehiring the boomerang for an appropriate opening that is legitimately available in your company.

- The boomerang may come back with a substantially higher salary, which may cause resentment among the coworkers who *didn't* leave the company or send the wrong message to the workforce that disloyalty is ultimately rewarded.

- And, perhaps most importantly, if there were unresolved issues that caused the candidate to leave in the first place, those issues may cause the boomerang to leave again—this time for good.

If the boomerang is a high-value candidate, none of these issues should be so insurmountable that you simply discount the value of returning employees. With a little planning and forethought, your network of high-value talent—both internal and external—will give you the advantage as you build a high-quality team of passionate employees who love their jobs and appreciate your company.

TRUTH

4

Rehire the retired

You thought your older employees would look forward to retirement and enjoy some time playing that extra round of golf or puttering in the garden. They did, too.

But many retirees are finding that a life full of leisure activities isn't as much fun as when these activities offered a break from the hectic pace of work. Many retirees are interested in returning to work, and so are their employers, who are discovering that certain skills and talents aren't readily available in the current talent pool.

When the Louisville Metropolitan Police Department (LMPD) faced labor shortages (they often have between 60 to 80 vacancies at one given time), they decided to look for innovative ways to staff open positions with experienced, qualified individuals. So, in May 2006, the LMPD hired 13 of its own retirees. Many LMPD retirees have 20 years or more of service. While they may have needed refresher courses and an update of their technical skills, they offered the LMPD a wealth of experience and background knowledge that was both invaluable and irreplaceable.

Police positions are hard to fill, not only because of the difficulty and risks associated with police work, but also because officers must have a passion and a drive for the work, according to Cheryl Wagner, the HR director for the LMPD. "By focusing on our retirees, we were able to tap into those people who have this work in their blood," she said.

For their part, these retirees are ready to go back to work after discovering that retirement left them bored and wanting interaction with peers and colleagues. People are living longer, and their bodies and minds are more youthful than when their parents hit retirement age 40 years ago. Today at age 65, life yawns large and long—and boring, not to mention expensive—once retirees discover they can play only so much golf. Retirees who happily return to their employers bring with them a refreshed sense of appreciation for the mission behind the work, as well as a seasoned perspective of the job and their roles within the company that could serve as a positive influence on their younger colleagues.

Many retirees are interested in returning to work.

Opening the door to retirees, either your own or those who've retired from other organizations, can be an excellent solution to some of your toughest staffing issues. Consider these strategies:

- **Keep in touch with your own retirees**—Not only can retirees help by bringing a historical perspective to current business problems during casual conversation, but you might also want to formally hire them back, either as permanent full-time, or to meet short-term project needs as temporary employees or consultants.

> Retirees who happily return to their employers bring a seasoned perspective of the job and their roles within the company that could serve as a positive influence on their younger colleagues.

- **Tap into other companies' retiree pools**—Look for organizations in your community that offer employment services for retirees. In many cities, AARP offers employment assistance and career counseling services to older job seekers.

- **Use resources offered by SCORE—the Senior Corps of Retired Executives**—This organization can help identify individuals with the talents and skill sets you need for long-term and short-term assignments.

Bringing back retirees is not without its own brand of challenges, however. Some retirees may not want the same hours or work demands, yet others may want equally demanding and challenging work. Some retirees may want to work on an *ad hoc* basis, offering their talents as needed by fluctuating job demands, while allowing them to enjoy months of leisure in southern climes, skiing trips to Vail, or in exploring the pyramids of Giza. Assume nothing. Talk with your retirees to determine what their needs are, and look for ways to reach win-win solutions.

TRUTH

5

Job-hoppers could be
show-stoppers

As you review the recent candidate's resume, you notice that he's remained with each employer for no more than two years at a time. "Not for me," you may think, remembering what you'd been warned about "job-hoppers" and their presumed unreliability. Job-hoppers used to be regarded as a hiring risk. They may not have a strong work ethic or may fail to offer loyalty to any employer. They may have rotten team skills or not be able to meet production goals. Or they soak up hours and hours of valuable training, at your expense, and then drift off to their next job, happily enriched by their new skills sets and experiences.

All that can be—and has been—true of people who change jobs frequently. Yet today's job-hopper may be different. Today's job-hoppers could be extremely ambitious, hard-working individuals who are driven to consistently hone their own competitive edge by working for companies that offer the training in the latest, most compelling techniques and technologies. If job-hoppers abound in your community or industry, it's up to *you* to make your company worthy of *them* and their ambition.

Job-hoppers, good or bad, may be all you have to select from. The U.S. Department of Labor reports that "job churn"—the number of people who voluntarily leave their jobs—grew at a rate of nearly 14 percent per year in the 1990s, doubling the rate of the previous decade.[1]

> Today's job-hoppers could be extremely ambitious, hard-working individuals who are driven to consistently hone their own competitive edge.

Often that churn is to the benefit of the hiring manager. Maybe you don't really need long-term tenures in some spots.

Consider one hiring manager who was looking for just the right person who could turn around a flagging sales team. The manager needed someone who knew the industry, knew the business, and most importantly, had experience in a successful turnaround. In walked the ideal candidate, who had several successful but short runs with similar employers in a turnaround situation. Who cares if he offers two years max to your team if he can get the job done? He still represents money well spent and time well invested.

> You may find that a savvy job-hopper who knows how to leverage his experience and gain

Such is the case with hiring managers today. You may find that a savvy job-hopper who knows how to leverage his experience and gain increasing job responsibility, credibility, and salary may be just the solution to your staffing need.

It's possible to distinguish savvy, valuable job-hoppers from ones who are just losers. Some clues for identifying savvy job-hoppers include progressive job titles, duties and responsibilities, and increasing salary. Or a plausible reason why there was a downward trend in salary or title (for instance, many executives take demotions to pick up valuable line experience, which will then position them for a better, faster career track a few years later). Have they stayed with an employer long enough to have made a valuable contribution? You might want to conduct a reference check and find out firsthand.

On the other hand, loser job-hoppers may say that they've moved for more money and to better themselves, but their job titles and compensation and benefits package may not confirm this story. Again, make the call and determine what the reality has been.

TRUTH

6

Seek refuge(e)

It would be easy to assume that the best recruitment talent pool would *not* be refugee workers. After all, they are new to this country and in an unstable, crisis-riddled phase of their lives. They may be unfamiliar with our customs, our language, and our employment practices and expectations. They might not own a car or even possess a driver's license. They may not have worked in your industry, or maybe they've worked in occupations that don't even exist in our country. They may be trying to learn many new tasks when they come to our country—from grocery shopping and cooking to finding mass transit routes and schedules, to completing necessary paperwork required by our government.

A *refugee* is defined by law as a person who "owing to well-founded fear of being persecuted for reasons of race, religion, nationality, membership of a particular social group or political opinion, is outside the country of his nationality and is unable to avail himself of the protection of that country." By definition, these are individuals who have no choice but to make a new life. There were 53,000 refugees admitted to the United States in 2005.[2]

Many hiring managers are learning that refugees may be one of the best labor pools from which to attract high-potential employees. They are often smart, independent thinkers—individuals who have fought persecution and overcome hardship to begin again in this country. In short, they are often motivated, hard-working, and conscientious workers.

One manager reports, "Before I hired refugees, I had a 60 percent turnover rate. Now I have 20 percent [turnover]. I had a 6 percent absentee rate; now it's down to .1 percent." Another manager who has found refugees to be a successful staffing solution says, "Since we began hiring refugees, our retention

They are often smart, independent thinkers—individuals who have fought persecution and overcome hardship to begin again in this country.

rate is 34 percent higher. Most new hires leave within a year. Refugees stay around four to five years," he notes. "Productivity rates are also higher. The refugees we've hired tend to do more volume more quickly." [3]

Another benefit is the diversity of cultural and language skills that refugees bring to the workplace. Refugees and their knowledge of world issues and possession of multiple languages can be a real asset, especially for hiring managers dealing with international issues.

> Before I hired refugees, I had a 60 percent turnover rate. Now I have 20 percent [turnover].

It's a mistake, however, to lump all refugees into a single category of survival-level need to work. Many refugees find that their skill sets are highly transferable, and they can get started with high-paying, complex jobs immediately. Others, however, recognize that until their language skills improve, or until they can receive their necessary professional credentials or certifications, they must start fresh in entry-level roles. It's not unusual, for instance, to find in some highly diverse communities a former college physics professor from Vietnam working as an apartment janitor.

Hiring managers who are interested in tapping into this labor market will find that working through refugee support organizations is the easiest and best way not only to identify key candidates and match them to open positions, but also to provide the support and encouragement often needed by hiring managers and refugee employees. These organizations provide both initial and ongoing training and support services, such as job-specific skill training, interpreters for interviewing and training, interpretation of training materials, and English as a Second Language classes. Most of these services are free to employers, making it even easier to tap into this labor market.

TRUTH

7

It's a war for talent

Two competing recruiters are on safari and come upon the path of a lion. The lion spots them; the recruiters freeze. Then one of the recruiters slowly begins to pull high-performance running shoes out of her backpack and puts them on. The other recruiter says, "You gotta be crazy; you can't outrun that lion." Her response: "Oh, I don't have to outrun the lion; I only have to outrun *you*."

In the war for talent, we are competing against each other for the best and the brightest. Even though we put all our energies into trying to chase down the best candidates for our open positions, we have to remember that a big part of the competition is outrunning other employers. It is, simply put, a jungle out there.

If the best candidates aren't working for your organization, they are probably working for your competitor. It's time for you to put on those running shoes.

Analyze your competitors

A first step is to identify who your competitors are for your first-choice employees. They aren't just your competitors for market share. They could be anyone, especially when you are looking for entry-level, hourly, and clerical workers.

For example, one fast food employer discovered that its competitors for employees included manufacturing (unskilled positions), hospitals (foodservice, housekeeping), banks (tellers), offices (entry-level administrative and clerical workers), almost all retailers (sales clerks, customer service reps), telecommunications and, of course, other restaurants and hospitality organizations.

Identify not only the competitors, but also the geographic region from which you recruit. For example, in rural communities, employers may need to identify employers within a 50-mile radius, or larger. Similarly, for organizations with very specialized roles, your competitors may be located across the country or across the globe.

Determine your marketing advantage

What does your organization have to offer in terms of the employment opportunity that your

It is, simply put, a jungle out there.

competitors don't, won't, or can't? In the marketing field, this is called your *unique competence*, or *unique selling proposition*. Consider this listing to determine which of these employment issues may best describe your most attractive message to potential employees:

- Organizational history

- Organizational stability

- Organizational culture

- Organizational physical attributes (state-of-the-art facility/equipment, comfortable facility)

- Size of the company

- Geographic locations of the company

- Training and educational opportunities

- Opportunities for advancement

- Direct and indirect compensation (salary and bonus)

- Benefits

    - Paid time off (vacation, leave, sick time)

    - Health insurance

    - Dental insurance

    - Vision insurance

    - Savings/retirement plans

    - Tuition assistance

- A participative and collaborative environment

- A product that employees are personally proud of

- Work/life opportunities (flexible work schedules)

- Safety issues

Craft your employment message that will "bag" those trophy candidates using all the advantages your company has to offer, beyond the simple paycheck. That's the way you can outrun your competition.

TRUTH

8

Maybe you don't want "new blood"

You keep hearing from managers, "We have to get some new blood." Your company seems to be suffering, perhaps, from doing things the same old way, and you need employees who can look at problems from fresh and innovative perspectives. It's natural to assume that the best way to get the best from your people is to look outside the organization. "We should get someone from a competitor or someone from outside the industry," you conclude. "That can help us turn this business around."

You look around at the employees already in your organization, and you think, "Kate's been here for five years as an admin, and she does a good job. But that's probably all she can do." And, "Jack has been great as the manager of receiving, but he can't handle the big job of plant management."

Maybe *you're* the one who could use some fresh thinking. Take another look at Kate and Jack. Internal candidates are often the ideal solution to a staffing need that requires a mix of new perspectives and company (or industry) knowledge:

- They already know the players, the politics, and the rules of the game. They don't have to learn your organization's culture and norms. They know the shortcuts to getting things accomplished quickly. They can hit the ground running.

- They are a proven commodity and have already demonstrated competence in key areas. You already know their strengths and weaknesses and how to manage these individuals to get their best output.

- They have some sense of loyalty and commitment, since they have continued to work for your organization. Many have a passion for the company and your products and services. They "get" you, and they believe that your company's mission is intrinsically important.

Internal candidates are often the ideal solution to a staffing need that requires a mix of new perspectives and company (or industry) knowledge.

- They feel recognized and rewarded for having been a good performer in the past, making them more likely to continue to perform at this level. Employees want upward mobility. You'll be helping morale not only by promoting these individuals, but also by demonstrating to their coworkers that commitment to growth and development is rewarded in your company.

- You can save a lot of money in external recruitment and on-boarding costs. If you have to hire externally to replace the person you've just promoted, the risk is lessened because it's now associated with a less valuable or specialized position.

Here is how you can identify key players who may be ready to move up, especially in larger organizations where you don't know all the players:

- **Use a job posting system**—If your organization has a job posting system, use it. In fact, some organizations may require you to use it as part of the recruitment process. Job postings include the job description and specifications.

- **Ask fellow managers to nominate key performers**—Some companies have a more closed approach and ask managers to nominate key performers to be considered for internal roles. Consider tapping your colleagues to determine if the talent you need is in their departments. Remember to return the favor when they come to you for nominations.

- **Consider opportunities for advancement within your department**—If you've been thinking only about your employees' capabilities in the light of their current duties and responsibilities, you might be thinking too narrowly. Maybe Kate is ready to move into a supervisory role, and Jack is ready to be tested in the role of plant manager. Identify ways to continuously develop your people so that they're ready for the next step. Develop a reputation in-house as a manager who

> Consider tapping your colleagues to determine if the talent you need is in their departments.

Assess whether your culture actually promotes innovation and change.

keeps the department employees' personal career futures in mind, and you won't have trouble with internal recruiting.

Finally, if you're looking outside your organization for fresh ideas and new ways of thinking, assess whether your culture actually promotes innovation and change. If employees are shot down every time they bring a new idea forward, they will quickly learn that new ideas aren't valued. Look inside your organization and how you respond to new ideas before first thinking that you need "new blood." Perhaps the old blood will be invigorated if you permit new ideas to flourish.

TRUTH

9

Your actions speak louder than words

You've invested huge amounts of money and time on your recruitment campaign. You have a beautiful, four-color recruitment brochure featuring why your company is one of the best places to work in the world. You sponsor some of the well-attended recruitment events in your industry. You feel proud that you have created an image that demonstrates your company as an "employer of choice."

But does it really pay off? Are you getting the best candidates?

Maybe not.

While you're spending large sums of money on fancy four-color ads, your employees are talking to their friends (your prospective employees) and telling them to stay away from your company. While you're serving cocktails and wining and dining the best and the brightest, your reputation on the streets is that you chew up and spit out good people. The bottom line: You have a bad image, since the buzz is that you're not a great place to work.

You don't give back to the community. You don't sponsor charities. You keep abusive managers while round after round of employees quit. The culture of your workplace punishes people who use the "liberal" leave and flextime policies that you brag about. In short: you don't live up to the image you've created as a great place to work.

If you can't actually be the employer that *keeps* workers, you can't be the employer that *attracts* top-notch applicants. The truth about who you really are and what you stand for will catch up with you—for good or bad. It all comes down to what people say about you based on their firsthand experience of how you treated them. Word-of-mouth communications about your organization can either help or hinder your formal recruitment strategy. In fact, in Nancy Ahlrichs' book, *Manager of Choice*, building and communicating a top-employer reputation is one of the cornerstones for becoming an employer of choice.

Beyond providing a work environment that is positive, there are many

> If you can't actually be the employer that *keeps* workers, you can't be the employer that *attracts* top-notch applicants.

other things you can do to build the image of your business as a great place to work. Here are a few:

> Let the community know when you and your employees are doing positive things within the community.

- **Send media releases about your employees and about your business**—Let the community know when you and your employees are doing positive things within the community. By putting your employee's name in front of the press, you are likely to establish a positive reputation as a good place to work. Ideas for articles might include a feature story on an employee who has just accomplished a major goal, such as completing a degree or returning to get a high school GED. It could be a story about an employee who was a hero. (For example, one employer notified the press about an employee who saw a house fire and rushed in to rescue two small children.) Other releases might provide information about the department's new commitment to training or ongoing education, or a brief on new benefits programs and other employee perks.

- **Be a good community citizen**—As the hiring manager, you might sponsor a Distributive Education Club of America (DECA) student through the local high school. Become a Little League sponsor. Participate in community activities, such as the Special Olympic Games. Encourage your employees to participate in the local walk-a-thon and provide T-shirts and hats to those who join. Invite the media to learn about your commitment to the community.

- **Develop your business network in the community**—Be a joiner and participate in community organizations and activities. Join the local Chamber of Commerce. Become active with the Rotary or Kiwanis clubs.

- **Be sure your employees know what you're doing to be a good place to work**—Let them know about your sponsorship of local events, about winning campaigns such as the "Best Places to Work" initiative, and about your charitable acts.

By creating a more positive image about your business, more employees will want to remain with your company. And, when more employees want to stay with your organization, you don't have to recruit as hard because your current employees stay longer and help build that good reputation in the community.

TRUTH

10

Targeting everybody attracts nobody

You want to attract lots of qualified candidates. So it's natural to think that the best way is to create a recruitment message to appeal to the masses. That way you'll have lots of responses and can choose from this large pool. That seems like a logical plan. There's only one problem: it's wrong.

Who do you get when you place your recruitment message with mass-market appeal? Nobody.

Your approach should be to aim very specifically at one narrow niche audience to get better responses. And these will be from an elite group of applicants who are truly best suited for the position.

Many marketing professionals have learned that to sell their products more effectively, they need to think of the specific kinds of customers who use their products and then appeal to them. You can borrow this targeting technique to directly appeal to specific groups of candidates. For example, one trucking company discovered that it had one position classification with very high turnover—its part-time driver position. The company decided that it would undergo an analysis to determine the causes. It learned that it had been attracting young people, who were accepting the part-time driver position in hopes that it would lead to a full-time role within the organization.

However, there was no career path from that part-time driver position, and it didn't make sense to create one. The department manager then studied the current employees with high rates of tenure and discovered that in those few instances where *older* workers had been hired, retention rates were excellent. The reason: older employees were not looking at this position as a stepping-stone. Therefore, this department manager decided to target older adults for these part-time positions. As a result, the trucking company attracted precisely the group of candidates who would be more likely to stay.

Another example comes from a major hospital in Mississippi. The nurse manager was hoping to

> Your approach should be to aim very specifically at one narrow niche audience to get better responses.

attract nurses with high retention rates, so she conducted a retention analysis to determine if there were any groups of nurses that had higher retention rates. She discovered that the nurses who were living in a community 75 miles away had excellent retention rates. This, on its face, seemed implausible. Wouldn't most nurses who had a 75-mile commute look for a job closer to home? The answer: the community had very high unemployment rates with no major hospital complex nearby. Therefore, the nurses from this community had a greater sense of loyalty toward their employer, even if their employer was a long commute away. As a result, the nurse manager decided to conduct a direct mail campaign targeting nurses in high unemployment communities within a 75-mile radius and was able to attract similar qualified and loyal employees.

If you are dissatisfied with the caliber of candidates, analyze the qualities and attributes of the long-term, productive employees you already have to give you valuable insights for targeting.

- Ask your top employees for ideas about attracting top candidates. Determine what the benefits of working with your organization are from *their* perspective and use these to target like-minded individuals.

- Study your turnover data and see if there are trends forming in certain areas or departments. Identify the reason for the turnover, and determine if the right candidates are being recruited for the right roles.

- Analyze your retention reports. Who are your long-term employees, and what do they have in common?

You may be wondering if targeting certain characteristics, such as gender or race, are permissible under law. The Equal Employment Opportunity Commission (EEOC), who handles these cases, has said

> If you are dissatisfied with the caliber of candidates, analyze the qualities and attributes of the long-term, productive employees you already have.

that managers may not be *exclusive* in their targeting messages, meaning that you can't say—directly or indirectly—that you are *only* interested in a particular protected category (say you're *only* interested in younger women or Hispanic candidates). The EEOC will also look at your overall recruitment efforts to determine if it is discriminatory—for example, if you are using an older worker recruitment strategy to offset your college recruitment efforts.

TRUTH

11

You are a talent scout

It's hard to find top talent. Consider the sports and entertainment industries that use talent scouts to identify outstanding potential players. The full-time job of a talent scout is to source, identify, and recruit talent for a team or organization. Similarly, if you're going to get the best talent in your industry, you constantly need to look for high performers and diamonds in the rough for players in your team. You are a talent scout for your department and organization. It's just that you're not going to sporting events and talent shows to spot the talent you need.

Where is the best place to talent scout? Consider where your target candidates are most often working, shopping, or going about their business. Sometimes you can find great employees at a local place of business—at a restaurant, pharmacy, dry cleaners, or department store—especially if you're looking for customer-service focused employees. For example, one large formalwear company provides talent scout cards (yes, that's what they call them) to all their managers. These cards are just a size larger than a traditional business card, with cutouts to allow the managers to insert their own business cards. The card announces that this formalwear company is always looking for people who demonstrate customer-friendly behaviors. When store managers or clerks meet a customer in the store who seems to have what it takes to be the kind of employee the company would like to have on board, they pass that person a card with the invitation to give the company a call.

A fast food company uses similar cards. These are bifold cards, with the cover saying "Caught ya," and the inside saying, "Doing service right!" The cards indicate that this organization is looking for service-minded individuals and that the recipient has been "caught." Just as with the formalwear company's cards, these cards then invite the recipient to use the contact instructions to find out more information about the company's opportunities.

If you're going to get the best talent, you constantly need to be looking for high performers.

If you're searching for professionals, they may be attending (or speaking at) a seminar, a meeting of a professional organization, or a conference, which may be the perfect time to talk about what your organization has to offer. You might want to take a promising contact to lunch, dinner, or drinks to discuss career opportunities at your company. You might even want to host a reception and invite key candidates to meet you and members of your organization during an industry or professional conference.

"Thanks for helping me! Does your employer appreciate your hard work?"

It's often hard to walk up to a would-be candidate "cold" without an opening line. Consider a *hook*—a way to get the candidate interested in your organization. You might begin by asking a question, such as

- "Thanks for helping me! Does your employer appreciate your hard work?"

- "Do you know of individuals who are looking for a chance to move up in their careers?"

- "Are you interested in learning more about some employment opportunities at my organization?"

- "Have you heard about all the exciting things we're doing at my company?"

All of these will serve as excellent ways to begin the conversation. Be ready, then, to talk about two or three advantages and benefits that your organization has to offer. "Close the sale" and ask to schedule an interview. By putting on your talent scout hat, you can get top candidates whenever you need them.

TRUTH

12

The Internet may not be the best place for recruiting

Modern candidates are looking at employers' Web sites and other employment sites to get the latest information on job openings. So, should you count more on the Internet, too? Not necessarily.

It all depends on whether your targeted candidates are primarily using the Internet as a tool for their job search.

For example, maybe your ideal candidates already have a job, love it, and aren't looking for a new one (*passive* job seekers). You can be pretty sure these passive job seekers aren't idly prowling through your Web site looking for opportunities in your company. Or maybe your population of employees and candidates just don't typically use computers outside of their limited work responsibilities. It's hard to believe in this day and age, but it's possible.

For example, one plant manager reported that his company had changed its recruitment strategy to posting all jobs on the Internet only, both on its own Web site and on some select employment sites. The result: virtually no responses. Upon further discussions with the plant manager's employees, the manager learned that most of its employees didn't own a personal computer and didn't have access to one.

While most people today do have at least some access to the Internet, they may not be using it to find jobs. And, if so, they certainly won't use it to find you.

Assuming your candidates are Internet savvy, consider the following:

- Consider using employment Web sites that are used by your target market. For example,

> You can be pretty sure passive job seekers aren't idly prowling through your Web site looking for opportunities in your company.

www.Monster.com may be a good source for young workforce entrants, but specialized and industry-specific Web sites may be better for attracting seasoned professionals in your industry. Craig's List (www.craigslist.com) could be a fantastic way to connect with newcomers to your community who are looking for their first job in their new town.

Consider using employment Web sites that are used by your target market.

- Include enough information about your organization, your culture, and the benefits you offer to entice candidates to check you out.

- Provide contact information so that the candidate can call or stop by your facility, since some may be unable to contact you if their access to a computer is at work.

- If you have any control over the keywords your company's computer is programmed to look for in online applications, make sure the list of keywords is as long and varied as possible. This way your own "net" will capture great candidate catches who otherwise would have slipped away.

Don't *just* rely on the Internet, even though it's working for you. You may know just the right candidate socially who is a perfect fit. Or your friend might have a friend who's perfect. But if you automatically turn to the Internet for the list of qualified candidates, an opportunity that arises during casual conversation with your friend could be completely lost.

TRUTH

13

Use the enthused

Could Joe, one of your sales reps, be a superhero in disguise?

A sales and marketing regional manager noticed that a number of recent recruits had something in common. Each had been referred to the company by Joe. When the manager asked one of the new employees how he knew Joe, the employee said he didn't really know Joe that well. Another said she had responded to an ad Joe ran.

Like many companies, Joe's had an employee referral program that gave cash rewards to employees who brought in new talent. While hopefully you won't have an employee looking to get rich through such a side business, having and encouraging such a program does reinforce one of the golden rules of recruitment: your best employees often have friends or contacts who can also be your best employees. Far from being a problem, Joe's entrepreneurial spirit turned out to be a blessing.

Joe's enthusiasm about the company led him to reach out to others. His message was simple and sincere: "Hey, this is a great place to work." It turned out, too, that the integrity of his enthusiasm was far more effective and cost effective than the sales pitches and recruitment methods standard to the company. Word-of-mouth recruitment can be the best kind, and Joe was living proof.

Employee referrals run on an engine of good will and the employees' self-interest. Studies show that almost half of employees view referring people to the company a good thing, as it both gives them a chance to help a friend and gives them the opportunity to work with people they know, trust, and respect. The employee referral mechanism also encourages employees to contribute to the shape of the company and leads to employees who are prone to stay. An Ohio State University study, for instance, shows that employees hired through referrals are 25 percent more likely to stay with the company than employees hired through other methods. Some aspects to consider:

"Hey, this is a great place to work."

- **Talk with employees**—Ask new employees specifically who the best and brightest are at their former company. Taking advantage of their network at their former company can help fill your open positions

> Encourage them to keep you informed of potential future candidates.

and those of others in your company. As your employees' and colleagues' networks expand, encourage them to keep you informed of potential future candidates.

- **Offer incentives and rewards that your employees value**—Instead of cash bonuses, some organizations offer electronics; some offer tickets to the team's home game. Others offer trips and high-ticket items, depending on the level of need and the difficulty of filling open positions.

- **Consider using employee referral during peak need periods**—If you are going into the Christmas buying season and need retail workers, you might offer a special incentive for those employees who refer friends during that time. For example, one retailer offered its regular employee referral incentive but added a drawing for all those who referred friends before the holiday rush.

- **Make the program easy to administer**—Many employers get into trouble by not paying on employee referral bonuses in a timely manner. Streamline a program that is difficult to administer because of multiple payouts or complicated rules.

TRUTH

14

It takes a village to hire one employee

Among the many problems involved with the job of finding a new employee, this one can stop you in your tracks: you don't have time to add hiring to your full plate of responsibilities. How can you squeeze in the very time-consuming job of replacing that employee when you're already so busy?

Answer: You don't have to go it alone. Your community, educational partners, and even the government can serve as recruitment collaborators who can help you source top candidates. Develop relationships with these key outside network contacts now, and they can help you beat the bushes to find the employees you need later.

■ **High schools**—Your local high schools may have excellent programs to prepare students for various clerical, technical, retail, sales, customer service, and entry-level roles. For example, Distributive Education Clubs of America (DECA) is an international association of high school and college students studying marketing, management, and entrepreneurship in business, finance, hospitality, and marketing sales and service. Developing relationships with DECA faculty can be an excellent way to reach top students with this emphasis of study.

Ask local schools if they have a career day where you might speak about careers in your company. Participate in career fairs sponsored by local high schools. Work with counselors, and select teachers to develop relationships so that they might recommend top students. Place an advertisement in the local high school newspapers, or post a notice on its Web site.

■ **Colleges, universities, and postsecondary schools**— Most managers find that they achieve the greatest success on college campuses when they identify those schools that yield the candidates who best meet their specific needs, and then develop a deep relationship with this small handful of schools. Some hiring managers target one or more schools

> Your community, educational partners, and even the government can serve as recruitment collaborators who can help you source top candidates.

based on the majors that they offer, for the kinds of students that they have (for example, some colleges attract more *nontraditional students*—older students who are already working), or for the location of the school (as when a manager knows the company tends to do best in attracting and retaining students with ties to the community).

> Talk with other employers in your community or industry to find out what national, state, and local resources they find to be the most helpful.

- **Government-funded agencies and programs**—Consider groups that support displaced homemakers, dislocated workers, disadvantaged youth, disabled workers, older workers, refugees, immigrants, and exiting military, to name just a few. Talk with other employers in your community or industry to find out what national, state, and local resources they find to be the most helpful.

- **Other employers—downsizing, rightsizing, relocating, opposite hiring needs**—Consider organizations that are downsizing, restructuring, relocating, or rightsizing—they may permit you to conduct an on-premises recruitment day or support your in-house promotion of a career fair or open house.

  Some employers within your community may have opposite hiring needs. For example, one company in Michigan that had peak-recruitment needs in fall and winter discovered another company in the same town who needed employees in the spring and summer. These businesses teamed up to offer full-time work and benefits, prorated between the two employers, increasing their ability to attract and retain loyal employees who can remain in their community as year-round residents.

- **Outplacement professionals**—Outplacement firms help employers provide support in job transition for executives, managers, and professional and technical employees who were caught in a downsizing or were not a good fit with the organizational culture or its future needs. Outplacement organizations generally receive a fee from the employer that needs to provide counseling for these individuals. And you can take advantage of the other employer's investment by letting these firms know of your recruitment needs.

■ **Realtors and relocation counselors**—Larger realty companies with corporate relocation services bring to your community executives, managers, and technical and other professionals who may have family members or trailing spouses who also need new jobs.

15

Newspaper ads can be great when managed properly

If you place an ad in the newspaper, you're really appealing to those who are looking for a job—*active job seekers*. But let's say you're mainly interested in attracting great, loyal employees who are already happy in their jobs—*passive seekers*—so you're tempted to abandon the newspaper ad approach. Be careful: you could be letting some great talent get away from you.

There are many great candidates who would love to be in the category of passive seekers. They have all those desirable attributes that passive seekers hold: loyalty, focus on the job at hand, stability. But there's one thing: they've just lost their jobs. And they're looking in the newspaper. And that's why you want to cover all your bases and place some recruitment messages (but not all) in the newspaper.

So, while newspaper recruitment advertising shouldn't be your only line of defense, it shouldn't be abandoned entirely. Use your paper well, and you will attract both passive and high-quality active seekers to your company's opportunities.

- **Go beyond the "Help Wanted" section**—Consider what sections your target market might read, such as the television, food, business, or sports sections. If, for instance, you want a mechanic, don't just place your ad under the M's in the classifieds. Buy a boxed ad in your paper's special editorial section devoted to cars.

- **Consider smaller newspapers**—Your local big city paper is usually the main source for job openings. But its target audiences could be as many as millions of people, scattershot around a large region. Excellent small-town papers, including local and community papers, can be a cost-effective way to use newspaper classified ads. There are fewer ads, and they appeal to locals. Your ad won't get lost.

- **Consider alternative papers**—The local business journal, service organizations' publications, health club newsletters, dining guides, "underground" entertainment newspapers, church newsletters, and even

Use your paper well, and you will attract passive and high-quality active seekers to your company.

convenience store bargain shoppers may be good low-cost options.

■ **Create news releases**—News releases are another way to let your target market know about employment and training opportunities. The big advantage here is that you won't pay to have news releases published in the paper. The big disadvantage is that you won't have control over whether the release will actually appear in the paper. And the announcement must be legitimate news—not just an ad in disguise.

■ **Write the ad enticingly**—To get the best response, *sell* your employment opportunities. Don't merely list the duties and responsibilities. Instead, consider the intrinsic and extrinsic benefits of working with your organization, and highlight these in your message.

If you have no savvy at putting pen to your message, you might want to hire a recruitment advertising agency or local freelance writer to create powerful, compelling messages.

As you develop your advertisement headline, use language that is strong, simple, and direct for the greatest impact. The words "you," "opportunity," "excellent," "exciting," and "new" are proven to be powerful words that attract readers. Avoid language that says you're desperate. "Help wanted" can be a red flag to someone seeking only high-quality opportunities. Testimonials and endorsements are powerful because they are messages from fellow employees.

As you develop your ad copy, keep in mind that specific and detailed messages have more impact than vague ones. An ad that features one position will get higher response rates from more qualified candidates than an ad featuring two or more positions.

When designing recruitment advertisements, consider clip-out coupons. These not only help attract interest, but they also offer another response option other than "apply in person" or "send resume to...."

> As you develop your advertisement headline, use language that is strong, simple, and direct for the greatest impact.

Borders can draw in the eye to create appeal for your message, or you might contrast your ad by using white space or reverse images.

So, don't abandon newspaper advertising, even when you're looking for passive job seekers. When managed properly, these ads can be powerful communication tools to get your recruitment message to your intended audience.

TRUTH

16

Your invitation might be chasing applicants away

You have an opening to fill. So you do what you've seen other neighboring businesses do: you put a sign in the window saying, "Help wanted. Apply within." Or you put a blind ad in the newspaper describing the position in broad terms and inviting all comers to send their resumes to a mystery company via mailbox.

Oddly, you receive no responses. Maybe the sign in the window wasn't visible enough. Or maybe next time, you should put a border around the classified ad in the paper—a nice thick line to attract the eye. Yeah, that's the ticket.

Don't bother. People are seeing the signs, all right. They're also reading between the lines. And your message has been saying to them, "We are such losers, we'll take anyone who comes in the door. Come work with us, and you can be a loser, too!"

Let's face it. The message, "help wanted" is pretty desperate sounding and not likely to draw in lots of wish-list candidates. Candidates who know their value look only for businesses that offer a value match. Wish-list candidates have a wish list of their own when it comes to the type of companies they want to work for. And first on their list is that their wish-list company isn't chronically desperate for help. Wish-list job seekers go after companies that have high-quality, well-thought-out employment strategies to get and keep the best employees on their team.

If you want to send the message that your company is the kind that high-quality candidates choose to work for, you have to behave like the kind of company that can afford to be exclusive and selective.

■ **The medium is the message—** Start by throwing away the "help wanted" sign and send out a different message instead. For example, one employer had been using a sign reading "help wanted," but no one came in to apply. So this savvy manager changed the sign to read, "Place your name on our employment waiting list."

> Let's face it. The message, "help wanted" is pretty desperate sounding and not likely to draw in lots of wish-list candidates.

The company was thus able to create an employment waiting list of actively interested—and supremely desirable—candidates who suddenly saw this company as a desirable place. It's not unlike the textbook marketing case in which Avis used the slogan "We're Number Two: We Try Harder" even though it was not number two but rose to the number-two position because of the positioning of this message.

> Try to create an invitation that appeals to the kind of employee you want in your company.

If you must blanket your town with a widespread invitation to apply, try to create an invitation that appeals to the kind of employee you want in your company. For instance, say you're an upscale stationery store and you want elegant sales staff who are passionate about good taste and knowledgeable about etiquette. Design a lovely window sign that almost looks like a wedding invitation, graciously inviting the honor of their presence at your daily celebration. Or you run a sports store and you need a sales staff that is chummy and fun with your customers. See if you can arrange to have some specially printed paper napkins with your job opening announcement to be handed out at your local sports bar. Use language that emphasizes the fun of your company's culture, and send that invitation to precisely the people most likely to RSVP with an application.

- **The *frequency* in any one medium is also the message**—Just like houses that have been on the market too long or last season's clothes still hanging in store racks, it's possible for job opportunities to get "shop worn." This is especially true when they're seen by the same people over and over and over again. This has a double negative effect: Not only is the current job devalued in the eyes of potential candidates, but your company gets the reputation of always being needy. Needy always looks suspicious—except, maybe, to needy candidates. You don't want needy candidates. Therefore, don't even think about rate holders in your newspaper (these are those small ads that appear daily and are very inexpensive) since they perpetuate a public image that you are always recruiting (thus, the reader believes, you always have staffing difficulties).

TRUTH

17

The candidate isn't the only one who has to interview right

Most candidates are a little nervous during the interview. There are so many ways they can mess it up. They can paint a not-so-rosy picture of themselves. They can forget your name. They can reveal too much information. Yes, candidates can certainly blow the interview and their chances for a great job.

You can blow the interview, too. And your mistakes can cost you much, much more. You may misread what the candidate says. You might ask questions that give away "correct" answers. Or perhaps you don't make the candidate comfortable enough to share candid information with you. Your own desperation to impress the ideal candidate could actually drive that candidate away.

In fact, there are many pitfalls you may encounter during the interview.

- **You don't establish rapport**—It is your responsibility to help the job candidate feel comfortable. Set the stage for the interview and help candidates feel so comfortable that they will tell everything about themselves—the good, the bad, and the ugly! Begin by asking a question to get the conversation moving, such as, "How were our directions? Did you find us without any problems?" or, "Can I offer you a cup of coffee?"

- **You do all the talking**—The 80-20 rule of interviewing should apply: you do 20 percent of the talking and let the candidate talk the remaining 80 percent. Unless you permit the candidate to share information, you cannot learn needed information that will assist in the selection decision. Resist the temptation to talk about the company, the position, and what you're looking for. You don't want to tip your hand or sell the candidate before you know you're interested in hiring that individual.

- **The interview questions are not prepared**—It's important to think through the information needed from the interview and have an outline of questions that you've jotted down in advance. If you're so distracted during the conversation

You can blow the interview, too. And your mistakes can cost you much, much more.

trying to think of your next question, you can't really hear those all-important answers. Many organizations have adopted a structured interview process, using the same basic interview questions for all job candidates.

- **The interview is too short**—A minimum of 20 minutes should be allotted for each job candidate, particularly for behavioral interviewing where past job examples are elicited to predict future performance. The optimum time for an interview is an hour or longer, especially for management interviews where many more job criteria are being measured.

- **You reach a premature decision**—If you make an instant decision upon meeting the candidate, such as on judgment of appearance, you could be missing out on hiring a great employee. Take the time to talk to all candidates, and give them the opportunity to sell themselves!

- **You experience the halo effect**—The *halo effect* happens when you hit it off immediately with a job candidate because, for example, you went to the same school. It's so easy to assume that those who went to your school, are from your hometown, or have the same favorite team will be wonderful employees. The opposite of the halo effect is sometimes called the *horn effect*. This happens when you see in the candidate something that is a pet peeve. For example, the last employee in the position (whom you had to fire) had an irritating habit—scratching his chin—and now the candidate sitting across from you exhibits the same irritating gesture. Guard against *both* the halo and horn effects in making good selection decisions.

- **You rely exclusively on intuition**—While you shouldn't ignore intuition, you should also guard against letting it rule your decisions without first finding out what the candidate said that made you feel comfortable or uncomfortable. Often our intuition kicks in and says "don't hire this candidate" because of a disconnect in what the candidate said and what the candidate's body language indicated at the time. For example, if the candidate said, "I'm really interested in this job," but said it with a flat tone of voice or with slouched or closed body posture, you may be receiving a mixed message.

18

Ask what they *will* do, not what they *can* do

Have you ever looked at a resume or application and just known you're going to hire this individual? *Wow, just look at this experience! It's perfect! And she has a degree in metallurgy, too!* Or have you ever interviewed a candidate and just known this is *the* one? *His experience is unique, yet so similar to our needs. He's worked in our industry. He even has some familiarity with our products. We gotta hire him now!*

And then, once you've hired an individual like that, you may begin to think, "I've hired the evil twin. Where did this stranger come from? This person isn't at all like the one I interviewed!"

What you may begin to realize is that you focused your time and attention—both in reviewing the application and the resume and in conducting your interview—on determining what the candidate can do, not about what he will do.

We know that just because a candidate *can* do the job doesn't mean he *will* do the job. Therefore, we need to search for two types of criteria: *can do* and *will do*.

Can do criteria are the objective measures that help us determine if the person has the knowledge, skills, credentials, and experience necessary to perform the job.

Will do criteria help us determine if the person has the drive, ambition, focus, and motivation to actually *perform* on the job. Will do criteria tend to be more subjective and include qualities and attributes.

Let's examine a hypothetical situation. You have two candidates who are somewhat matched in terms of both the can do and will do factors. Candidate One is a little stronger in terms of can do criteria, and Candidate Two is a little stronger in terms of will do criteria. Who will you hire?

Most managers indicate they would rather hire the will do candidate—Candidate Two—because they can teach someone who is a bit deficient on can do factors by providing

> We know that just because a candidate *can do* the job doesn't mean he *will do* the job.

on-the-job training or development. But it is nearly impossible to change someone who does not have the motivation, attitudes, or competencies required for the job. That's one of the reasons why it's important not to think of these criteria as "soft skills"—they are at least as important—if not more so—than hard skills.

Many managers tend to be frustrated in the hiring process because they've focused only on the can do factors and have failed to ask good will do questions. So why don't managers just ask better questions?

One reason is that it's hard to ask about will do criteria, especially in any sort of direct way. For example, if you ask candidates, "Are you creative?", what are you likely to hear? Chances are you'll never hear a candidate say, "Oh gosh, creativity, no, that's not me."

Another way that managers have traditionally tried to ask will do questions is by asking hypothetical questions—"what if" questions, such as, "What would you do if you were dealing with a difficult customer?" as these help determine will do qualities indirectly.

But there is a problem with hypothetical questions: if you ask a hypothetical question, you get a hypothetical answer. You don't hear what the person really *would do*, just what he believes to be the correct answer. (Keep in mind, though, that when you ask a hypothetical question and you receive a terrible answer, you have learned the person doesn't even know what the correct answer should be—which is important information to know!) But, individuals who answer the question correctly may not have acted that way in the past, nor is it guaranteed that they would use this same judgment in the future.

We know from industrial psychologists that the best predictor of future performance is past performance. One way to get a more accurate picture of what the candidate truly is capable of— especially in the areas that require judgment or self-motivation—is to ask applicants to tell a story of how they have handled similar issues

> But there is a problem with hypothetical questions: if you ask a hypothetical question, you get a hypothetical answer.

in the past. What were their *behaviors* when faced with a related challenge?

Begin with words or phrases such as, "Think of a time when you had to...", or "Consider an example when you...", or "Relate a story about when you...".

By asking behavioral interview questions, you can better to discern the great candidate from the one with the "evil twin."

19

Charlie might be more than just a great mechanic

You've just interviewed Charlie for your lead mechanic position. He knows what low voltage from the oxygen sensor means. He knows how voltmeters are hooked up in a circuit. He can just touch his hands to the engine and know what needs to be fixed without even looking. He is an A-1 mechanic, and you desperately need an A-1 mechanic. So naturally, you offer him the job.

When he gets on the job, he proves that he can do the work. However, you're learning other things about Charlie. Fellow mechanics believe that he has stolen their tools. He often comes to work with alcohol on his breath. He swears in front of customers and has already alienated one of your best customers. You catch Charlie in several lies. You ultimately have no choice but to fire Charlie, even though he is technically one of the best mechanics you've ever seen.

Just because a mechanic knows how to fix a car doesn't mean he will be a good employee. It takes a lot more than just the knowledge and skills to do the job. And yet we're often eager to make job offers to candidates who we know possess the skills and experience we need without exploring all the other issues that determine whether that employee will be successful on the job.

This is especially true when you have positions that are highly technical or specialized, have unusual skill set combinations (for example, a CPA who is fluent in Japanese), or for difficult-to-recruit-for areas (small rural communities, for example), industries, or positions. It's easy to become so focused on the fact that the candidate has the unusual skill sets that you fail to explore other issues. Or, you may find that when you learn that the candidate is willing to work in your middle-of-nowhere location, you make an offer on the spot.

Another issue is that while you may intuitively know that work ethic and integrity are important qualities, these may be hard to determine in the interview. If you ask candidates if they have a strong work ethic and a high level of integrity, they don't have to be a genius to know what the right answer is. And yet, by asking the right questions, hiring managers can determine these important elements that are crucial to ultimate job success.

It takes a lot more than just the knowledge and skills to do the job.

Consider these questions:

- Tell me about a time when you helped a coworker. What did you do, and how did it turn out?

- Tell me about a situation where you saw something that needed to be done outside of your duties and responsibilities, but you did it anyway.

- Tell me about a time when you had a disagreement with a supervisor, coworker, or customer. What did you do? What happened?

- Tell me about a time when you had to be courteous to someone at work who really didn't deserve it.

In addition to listening for candidates' responses to these questions, you might also listen for other clues that speak to their work ethic.

- Do they have favorable things to say about their supervisor, coworkers, and their last employer?

- Do they seem upbeat and genuinely interested in the job?

- Are they *only* asking questions about time off and vacation, or do they ask these questions first before ever asking about other elements of the job?

- Do they demonstrate courtesy throughout the interview? (For example, do they thank the interviewers for their time? Do they write thank-you notes?)

  As you did to determine work ethic, you can ask specific questions determining the integrity of a candidate. These questions focus on issues such as attendance, punctuality, performance, honesty, illegal drug and alcohol use, and criminal behavior.

- What do you consider to be acceptable tardiness/attendance?

- Tell me about a time that you were counseled by your supervisor. What did you learn?

- What are the reasons that you left your last employers?

■ If I were to call your supervisor, what would I learn about your performance?

■ We're going to conduct a thorough background check. Is there anything I need to know?

■ A drug test will be required before you can start to work. Will there be any problems?

In addition to listening for candidates' responses to these questions, you might also consider using background and reference checks, paper and pencil honesty testing, and drug testing to determine integrity.

TRUTH

20

Passion—in fashion?

Let's face it. When people talk about what they're really passionate about, they tend to forget everything they learned in the "what to say when you're interviewing" self-help books. All those buttoned-down corporation-speak responses go right out the window as their true excitement lights up their eyes. It can actually be a little scary at times (especially when that excitement reminds you of someone you once knew—yourself maybe?). Don't call the interview to a quick conclusion! Open it up even more to find out what really lights the candidate's fire. Then, if the fit seems right, take a deep breath and offer that person the job.

Find out about the candidate's work-related passions. If a candidate today isn't passionate about the industry, the profession, or the company, you're probably going to be dealing with an employee who will become quickly disengaged and unmotivated once she gets used to that steady paycheck.

If you have a passionate employee who believes that what she's doing is an essential task, you have an employee who doesn't need external motivation. She is already wired to do what's necessary to get the job done, since she believes that the job is Job One in both her heart and her mind.

Most of us want to work with a team of people who believe in their work and that they can make a difference. These people are easier to manage, especially when you keep showing them how they continue to live a life of purpose through their work. They're also easy to spot.

- **Ask candidates about what gets them excited to come to work**—Ask them to tell you about the last time they were so engrossed in their work that the day just flew by. Ask them about a time when they woke up and were glad it was Monday and not Friday.

> If you have a passionate employee who believes that what she's doing is an essential task, you have an employee who doesn't need external motivation.

- **See how personally knowledgeable your candidates are about your product, industry, market, or customer base—** For example, those considering a career in the publishing field should be able to talk about the books they're reading and be ready to discuss why they chose these books. Container Stores intentionally recruit from their own community of regular customers on the theory that anyone who gets excited about organizers and cleaning supplies enough to frequently return to the store would likely be enthusiastic evangelists for the company itself.[4]

  Or take the example of a receptionist at a law firm who believed she had the most important job in the company. She said that she had always been told that her gifts were a sunny disposition and the ability to make people's day, and that she was in a job that allowed her to use those gifts and make a difference. She said that she had the ability to brighten the day of all the people who visited the firm and who called to speak to one of their attorneys. That's the kind of person you want on your team.

- **When asking about the applicants' last job, observe their energy level and animation while talking with you—**Are they obviously excited and energetic when talking about their work? Do their eyes light up and get that twinkle of excitement?

- **Ask about candidates' last work assignments, and listen to the words they use to describe their work—**Do they talk about how much they love their work? Do they comment on how they are passionate about what they do for a living?

- **Ask candidates why they want to work for this company, in this department, and in this job—**If they can't answer the question, they probably don't have the passion to do the work. Or if they answer in terms of *my* career, *my* salary, *my* benefits, you also understand their motivation. Listen for those candidates who have an understanding of their unique gifts and how those gifts and talents can be put to use for a purpose in the work you're providing.

21

Good candidates might not talk to you

Great candidates can be terrible interviewees. They may not have had a lot of experience in interview settings precisely because they are such great employees. If they have a track record of getting snapped up by eager employers, they may simply not have the skills and practice to put themselves out there conversationally. Or maybe they're shy. Or nervous. Or they have had test anxiety in the past, which now translates itself into interview anxiety. Keep in mind that you have had far more experience interviewing people than your candidates have. So, unless you're hiring a public speaker or game show host, don't look for outgoing conversationalists.

Getting a quiet, shy, introvert to open up and talk with you can be a challenge. And it can be especially challenging if you are also a shy introvert who would rather be doing anything but interviewing a long string of candidates, only one of whom is actually destined to get a job. Still, you have to be personally, energetically, and authentically interested in each and every one of them. Even though most of them would rather be doing anything but interviewing with you. Keep in mind that in this setting, you're the host. So it's up to you to help the candidates do their best.

■ **Ask open questions that require lengthy answers revealing something about the applicant's personality or experience—** Excellent questions designed to draw out the candidate are

   ■ Why are you interested in applying for this job?

   ■ Compare your past role with the one you're interviewing for here.

   ■ Describe a typical day.

Most any question that begins with *how*, *why*, *compare*, or *describe* are open questions that will elicit a lengthier response.

■ **Ask general approach questions**—These are broad, open-ended questions—usually "tell me about" questions. Listen for how candidates frame their

> Unless you're hiring a public speaker or game show host, don't look for outgoing conversationalists.

responses. For example, general approach questions might include, "Tell me about your last supervisor," or "Tell me about your educational background." These are job-related questions that prompt the candidates to expand on some important element of their background or experience.

> It's not your job to personally like the candidates because of their gift for sparkling conversation.

- **Ask evaluative questions**—These are questions that ask the candidates to describe how they judge some aspect of their past performance or experience, such as, "How would you rate your past experience?"

- **Remain open and nonjudgmental**—The more you can remain open and nonjudgmental, the more likely candidates are to share all the details of their past, even the unsavory parts. Keeping whatever judgmental thoughts you might have to yourself can help candidates relax and reveal even more.

- **Use paraphrasing or mirroring techniques**—These are techniques that psychologists commonly use to draw out additional information and insights from their clients. By *paraphrasing* what candidates just said, you are giving them the chance to hear themselves through your voice and words and elaborate on some detail that you might have missed. *Mirroring*—copying their mannerisms or posture—however, is a technique to help candidates relax because subconsciously they begin to identify with you. This is used to get the individual to open up and provide more details.

- **Use silence to your advantage**—It's human nature to fill up the silence void with talking. In the interview setting, it's much better to use silence to *your* advantage, especially when you want the applicant to elaborate on the answer provided.

There are many ways to pry the shy guys out of their shells. The hard part for you is simply to remember that it's not your job to personally like the candidates because of their gift for sparkling conversation. You're hiring for skills, experience, and culture fit. The personality may blossom once they're comfortably onboard.

TRUTH

22

You're not Sigmund Freud

The rise of pop psychology in the 1960s created a new phenomenon in the 1990s: the pop psychology interview. As managers grew increasingly interested in refining their selection techniques, it became trendy to throw some curveball questions to candidates to see what their answers would reveal. Soon they became commonplace—regardless of whether they were actually valid or job related.

Managers often have a pet question, usually one in which they "play psychologist." These are questions such as, "What is your favorite color?" "What was your favorite class in school?" "If you could be any animal of the forest, what would you be?" or even, "Which of the Seven Dwarfs best describes your personality?" (No kidding, this is a recent "playing psychologist" favorite!) You might have your own pet questions—the ones you think give you incredible insight to the innermost thoughts, motivations, and behaviors of candidates.

There are several problems with each of these types of questions:

■ They are not job related, which may cause issues of discrimination.

■ There is no one "right" answer.

■ Interviewers are not, by and large, rigorously trained psychological researchers. So they don't know what they're doing and they wouldn't know what to do with the answers to these questions— even if those questions were otherwise legitimate.

What is the right answer to the favorite color question? Is it red (your candidate shows latent aggression or at least extroversion) or green (your candidate likes money)? Is it white (serene and peace seeking—at least in Western cultures) or black (the color of death, unless you're in Japan, where the color of death is white)?

Benchmarking responses

There is one way to peer into the mind of your applicants to see how they tick. Create "benchmarked responses"—ideal responses you

Managers often have a pet question, usually one in which they "play psychologist."

expect to hear from ideal candidates. For example, if you ask the question, "Tell me about a time you had a disagreement with one of your coworkers," decide in advance what might constitute a "good" or "ideal" response.

- I listened to her side of the argument, realized that I was wrong, and apologized.
- I explained why I acted the way I did, and we patched up the disagreement.
- We worked together to find consensus around the disagreement.
- I lead the group in a discussion to find different options for the problem.

Now, consider what you would decide might constitute "bad" or less-than-ideal responses. These might include

- We never did see eye to eye.
- We had a huge fight, and the manager had to referee.
- I ended up not speaking to the team for several weeks.
- We sabotaged one another in our work. It was horrible. That's why I'm looking for a new job.

It's important, however, to keep in mind that there are many answers that are neither positive nor negative:

- We needed a third-party—in this case our manager—to help us get back on track.
- We agreed on one way of handling the situation, but no one was really pleased with the outcome.
- We barely spoke to one another or had lunch together, but we continued with our work.

Once you have identified positive, negative, and neutral responses, you now know what to look for when you ask an interview question.

Study the behaviors of your top performers and outline the key behaviors that make them part of your "A" team.

To identify appropriate benchmarks, study the behaviors of your top performers and outline the key behaviors that make them part of your "A" team. This can be accomplished by examining performance appraisals, by talking with employees in position, and by observing their daily actions.

Using benchmarks during the interview

After you develop a series of benchmarks for specific questions or groups of questions, create a system for rating candidate responses. This is often done by using an interview guide—developed by the hiring manager to ensure the same questions are asked of all candidates for the same position. One employer has developed a guide for its hiring managers that includes benchmark responses for each category of questions used. For example, around "customer service orientation," it has a series of questions that might be asked for this competency, followed by benchmark responses with a box for each category of responses.

TRUTH

23

Candidates and the truth—the whole truth

Interviews are about more than just asking really good questions and then listening and assessing answers. Those answers may be only half-answers, giving you only part of the entire picture behind the candidate's response. Sometimes candidates will share only limited information, knowing that the whole truth may cost them the job offer. Or their intent may be simply more innocent: They don't realize that they're not giving you the whole truth, because they're operating on the assumption that you know more than you do. Or they simply don't know that the critical details are in the answers they give. Regardless of their motivations, the job is yours to get the truth—the whole truth. Therefore, asking probing follow-up questions is critical.

Don't take answers at face value. Probing and follow-up questions can reveal more than the candidate's initial answer. Candidates may need your help in showing you the entire picture.

One way to assess whether you have the entire picture is to listen for what's missing. There may be times that the candidate tells you the background and the action taken, without telling you the results. Or the candidate may share details of the action taken and the results but fail to set up the situation or background.

It's important to understand the context for any example or story the candidate shares. If you don't have the background, you don't understand if the action taken was appropriate or how similar or dissimilar it is to your work situation. When the background is not clear, probe a little more by saying, "Give me a little of the background," or "What led up to this?" or "What brought this on?"

It's also important to understand the candidate's behavior. You should have a clear picture of the action taken within the context of the situation or background information. You'll also want clarity on who, specifically, took the action. For example, was the action taken by the candidate alone, or the candidate's team? When the

> Don't take answers at face value. Probing and follow-up questions will reveal more than the candidate's initial answer.

behavior is not clear, ask, "What specific actions did you take?" or, "How did you do that?"

You also need to get a picture of the outcome or results of the candidate's action. Without knowledge of the outcome, you may not learn that the candidate's action was inappropriate or cost the company money. When candidates are sharing a story or an example from their work history, you want to know about the outcome. In those cases when the result is not clear, ask, "What was the result?" or, "How would you rate the action that you took?"

There may be times when a candidate leaves unanswered questions about some of the details. In these cases, you may want to ask a very focused and even use a closed question to get the specific information you need.

For example, the candidate has just given you some general information about his educational background, and you still need more details. You might ask one of these closed follow-up questions.

- What other on-the-job training did you receive at your last job?

- In what field did you excel?

- Have you used your education on your past job?

You might also ask for more open responses when you have general questions to be answered.

- Tell me more about some of the supervisory development you received.

- How did you go on to apply that knowledge?

- What was it about that instruction that got in the way of performing your job duties?

- Can you elaborate on your education?

> You can get valuable information from the answers the candidate doesn't provide—namely, red flags.

■ Please tell me about another example when that happened.

■ What else do I need to know to help me in making this decision?

You can get valuable information from the answers the candidate doesn't provide—namely, red flags. For example, when a candidate says, "I always double check all my work to make sure it's accurate," you know that this is not a specific example because he said, "I always." Therefore, "always" becomes one of the red flag words to help identify these issues. Other red flag words in responses include "I never" (this does not indicate a specific example), "We did…" (this indicates behavior of a team, not an individual), or "I try to…" (this isn't what the individual actually did; it's what this person attempted).

TRUTH

24

Don't let the candidate's resume drive the interview

Everyone knows that resumes are an essential tool in most selection scenarios. Yet most of us would also agree that candidates receive lots of coaching about how to put together their resumes, from which items to put first to which achievements to highlight and what competencies to underscore. There are executive coaches and job placement professionals who make good money providing this advice to your applicants. In fact, you might have received professional help getting your resume into shape for your own last job hunt—probably for the job you have now.

So it wouldn't surprise you to hear that many candidates tailor each resume they send out to meet the exact specifications outlined in recruitment ads they're responding to—including your own announcement. Most candidates have their "standard" resume on their home computer, and they merely tweak it based on the language they see in the ads that catch their eye. So you really shouldn't be completely shocked when the resume on your desk seems to magically fit the requirements you've outlined for the job in your recruitment message.

It's not magic; it's Microsoft Word. And if you spend too much time reviewing the resume with the candidates sitting in front of you, you have just given over your power of discernment. Put the resume down and move away from the paper. You shouldn't be reading in front of guests anyway.

Here are some ways to outsmart the resume so the resume doesn't outsmart you.

- **Review the application, resume, and prescreening interview notes before the candidate shows up for the interview—** The written materials have already done their job: they've provided the necessary data to convince you that the candidate should be interviewed. On a separate sheet of paper, jot down the important background facts to go over with the candidate (as well as any possible red flags, such as frequent job changes or gaps in employment history), and then put the original set of documents away.

It's not magic; it's Microsoft Word.

- **Depend on your conversation with the applicant to determine whether that person's background is a match with the job requirements**—Is the candidate's background relevant to the requirements of this current job opening? If the position carries with it any specific expertise or jargon, listen for whether the candidate comfortably uses those words or can give examples of how he put that necessary expertise into action.

- **Listen for how the candidate talks about previous workplace experiences and bosses**—Most of the stories and examples should be generally positive, with happy and successful endings. The candidate's comments about previous bosses should also be positive. They don't have to be glowing, and all the stories don't have to be 100 percent upbeat. Just listen for whether the candidate's answers reflect a strong sense of self-empowerment or a consistent theme of victimization. Without a resume in front of you to distract you, you can listen more carefully, not only to the answers but also to the tone of those answers.

- **Listen for "prefab" answers**—It's possible for responses to sound too perfect. In fact (and ironically), the better you wrote the position vacancy announcement, the more you are at a disadvantage at this stage of the selection process. A clever, but unqualified, candidate will have absorbed the language and the qualifications, only to parrot them back to you as if from his own experience, skills, and history.

- **Focus your attention fully on what the candidate is saying and what his body language is**—Without the distractions of the candidate's carefully prepared pieces of paper, you can pick up the subtleties of insincerities.

Put the documents away, and claim the driver's seat.

Put the documents away, and claim the driver's seat.

TRUTH

25

Avoid the "hot seat"

"Hey, we've got a very stressful environment," you may be saying. "We need to be sure our employees can handle stress."

Your environment may indeed be highly stressful. Your salespeople may need to work with irate and abusive clients. Your security guards may log hair-trigger incidents on a weekly basis. Perhaps your employee assistance counselors are booked into the next millennium. Or maybe your overall culture carries with it a rough-and-tumble environment that requires a bit of a thick skin. The very nature of your business brings with it supreme stress. So it only follows, you think, to be able to test the capacity of your candidates to function in high-tension environments.

Your organization might be guilty of hot-seat interviewing, and you may not even know it. You're so accustomed to this pressure-cooker environment that behaviors other employers would consider to be firing offenses barely cause a ruffle in your office. Still, for the sake of finding out how potential employees can withstand the stress of your environment, your company has instituted some mutton-headed ways of sniffing out the crybabies.

- Panel interviews are designed to keep the candidate disoriented and confused. There's no clear leader of the panel; no one is sitting at the head of the table or in the center, where the chairman would conventionally sit. Some companies even position panelists behind the candidate. After the candidate is sufficiently disoriented by the physical arrangement, the panelists become increasingly abusive and disrespectful to see how the interviewee handles this behavior in a professional setting.

- The interviewer purposefully demonstrates rude behaviors, such as allowing a candidate to wait (sometimes for hours), smoking and blowing smoke into a candidate's face, or placing a candidate in an uncomfortable chair. (There are even stories of managers who intentionally use a very low chair for an interviewee so that they can tower over a candidate,

Your organization might be guilty of hot-seat interviewing, and you may not even know it.

and other stories of managers using a chair for the interviewee with one leg much shorter than the other.)

■ Candidates are subjected to yelling, abusive language, and overtly aggressive behaviors.

These are very informative tactics, to be sure. They tell the candidate that this is the wrong place to work.

These are very informative tactics, to be sure. They tell the candidate that this is the wrong place to work. Any candidate who sticks around after that kind of treatment is either desperate for a job or mentally unbalanced.

You *do* need to determine if a candidate can handle the stresses inherent in the job, but being rude or abusive during the interview is not the way to go. In today's environment where good candidates are hard to come by, you don't want to chase away great prospects by demonstrating rude, abusive, or manipulative behaviors. If stress is an important element of the job and you would like to see how a candidate might handle it, it is much better to ask a behavioral interview question that determines how she handled stress in a past work situation.

■ "Tell me about a time when you had multiple projects with converging deadlines. How did you handle it?"

■ "Tell me about a time when you had to deal with a particularly abusive customer. What was your response?"

■ "Tell me about a time when you had a major conflict with your supervisor, team member, or subordinate. Tell me about it and how you dealt with that situation."

If your work environment insists on celebrating behaviors that make *Rambo* look like *Romper Room*, it's time for you to start looking for a new job yourself. As long as you stay there, you're absorbing bad behavior habits that can make you look bad in your own interviews.

TRUTH

26

You *can* oversell the job

You've just interviewed the thirty-seventh candidate for your open position. You are sick and tired of interviewing. Your team is about to picket because it's been forced to work overtime. You desperately want this candidate to be "it."

You look carefully at the resume and application. The work history is strong—this candidate has even worked in the same industry. Wow, look at the strong credentials that this candidate offers! We gotta get him! But how? The last candidate was unimpressed with what we had to offer and even scoffed at our salary range and benefits package. Maybe all we need to do is to really talk up what we have to offer...perhaps even fudge a little on our opportunities and training. If we can get this candidate to take our offer, what harm could there be with a little stretching of the truth?

Chances are, especially in this labor market, you have been desperate to fill a position—maybe even to the point of being tempted to inflate the value of the opening to candidates. But just as you don't want candidates who overpromise and then underdeliver, you don't want to give into the temptation of setting candidates up for a disappointment. The consequences will cost you.

When new employees discover their job isn't as rewarding as the picture you've painted, they become disgruntled and leave the organization. Or just as perplexing, new employees discover their job isn't as rewarding as the picture you've painted, and they become disgruntled employees and *stay*! In this second scenario, they wreak havoc on employee morale, they offer diminished productivity, and they may even sabotage the organization. (These are "actively disengaged" employees.) You may ultimately have to fire these individuals and begin the hiring process once more.

In either case, you're lowering productivity and morale, and having to begin the hiring process again.

> Chances are, especially in this labor market, you have been desperate to fill a position—maybe even to the point of being tempted to inflate the value of the opening to candidates.

And each time you cycle through another mismatch, you're driving up the costs of hiring the eventual perfect candidate who is still out there waiting for a great job.

You can take steps to counteract your own natural urge to fill positions by inflating the value of the job through an understanding of what behaviors you might exhibit when you begin to feel desperation creep into your recruitment efforts.

- You talk too much about what the organization has to offer instead of asking great questions to determine if the candidate is worthy of being sold.

- You ask leading questions, giving candidates clues to appropriate responses.

- You make offers on the spot instead of carefully evaluating candidates with time-consuming but essential tools such as background and reference checks.

- You over-promise some term or condition of employment, such as salary, benefits (including more vacation or shorter eligibility period), or working conditions.

Strategies to avoid overselling

- **Use a predeveloped interview guide**—By using the interview guide that you developed in less urgent times, you won't be as tempted to ask leading questions or to spend too much time selling instead of asking good interview questions.

- **Use a check list covering the selling points your organization offers**—Before the interview, develop a list of the selling points you have to offer and review this list with the candidate. Don't stray.

- **Don't promise anything before thinking through the potential repercussions**—If you're considering offering a salary that is higher than your range, consider whether you're willing to adjust salaries, or if you're willing to risk losing your current team when word gets out that the newbie is making more than the team.

- **Don't make offers on the spot**—Give yourself a cooling-off period before extending an offer. Check references and background information. Be careful not to tip your hand with comments such as, "You're definitely the best candidate, and I'm sure we'll be making you an offer."

Remember that there's a difference between overeager and enthusiastic. Candidates who see you as being overeager will be wondering why you're desperate. Candidates who see you as enthusiastic will be congratulating themselves for how well they've sold themselves to *you*.

TRUTH

27

There is such a thing as a bad question

Questions are good. We learn when we ask questions. We gain new insights when we query others. We obtain a new understanding of the world in which we live by asking.

We also know that when we work with others that asking questions helps us do a better job as team members. Questions help us clarify work assignments, outline the tasks involved, and explore unforeseen variables together.

Yet, there definitely are some bad (as in downright dangerous) questions when it comes to preemployment interviewing. You may think you're asking an insightful question, but the question may not be job-related and, therefore, may not provide you with the job-related information you need to make an informed decision. Or you may want to ask questions that get at the candidate's psyche, when in reality you have no clue as to what the right answer is.

Outlined here are types of counterproductive questions and ways to reword or reframe them to make them better for employee selection.

■ **Questions that are not job related**—Irrelevant questions are worse than being simply uninformative. They also waste time and give the candidate the impression that you haven't done the necessary preparation for the meeting. You might just lose a candidate, who decides that your opportunity isn't her "A" opportunity. Questions of this variety include ones like, "What do you like to do most in your spare time?" or "What are the things you care most about?"

Better questions include these:

■ Tell me about your relevant educational and work experience.

■ Do you have any hobbies or outside interests that are relevant to this job?

■ What have you liked most about past employment experiences?

There definitely are some bad (as in downright dangerous) questions when it comes to preemployment interviewing.

- **Questions where there is no right answer**—These are often questions in which managers "play psychologist" to gain valuable "insights" into the way the candidates tick. These are usually not effective because 1) the manager is not a psychologist, and 2) the manager really doesn't know what a right answer would be. Examples include questions like, "What is your favorite color?" or "What is the most important thing about being successful?"

  Better questions might include these:

  - What is your motivation for seeking this position?
  - Tell me about a time in which you had to work in a dysfunctional team. Be specific.
  - Tell me about the steps you took to complete a project successfully.
  - Tell me about a conflict you had with your manager and how you resolved it.

- **Questions in which you invite a false answer**—If you are asking the candidate directly if she possesses some quality or competency, you may be inviting a false answer. No one readily admits to not having a quality that you obviously (by asking a question) have deemed important to the job. Samples of these direct questions that tend to invite false answers include, "Are you creative?" or "Do you usually arrive for work on time each day?"

  Better ways to ask about these issues might be as follows:

  - Tell me about a time when you had to come up with a creative solution to a difficult and unique problem.
  - What do you consider acceptable attendance?
  - In your previous job, how many days in a month/year were you late for work?

- **Leading questions that hint at what you consider to be acceptable answers**—Don't give clues as to what the correct answer is, as in the following questions: "Did you apply for this job because you were looking for a way to advance in your career?" or "Did you not receive satisfactory ratings from your last supervisor because she was jealous of you?"

Here are better ways to ask about these issues:

- What would your last supervisor say about you if I were to call?
- How would you rate your job performance?
- Tell me about a time when you didn't do well in your job. What happened, and what did you do?

TRUTH

28

You're guilty until you prove you're innocent

If you go to a cocktail party and meet a dark-complexioned woman who is dressed in a sari and speaks with a heavy accent, it is perfectly normal and socially acceptable to ask, "Where are you from?" Or say you go to a dinner party and meet a handsome man. After you subtly shift your eyes to his left hand, you note that he isn't wearing a wedding band (and you're single and looking). You might be tempted to ask, "Are you married?" If a woman you meet at church is wearing a charm bracelet with pictures of her children or grandchildren, you could take that as an invitation to ask her about her family.

Asking those questions in social situations aren't necessarily landmine moments. But asking those same questions in an interview setting could cost you millions of dollars—if not your job. Yes, you want your candidate to relax. And, yes, your skillful, seemingly casual questions could reveal some important facts about the candidate. But they could also result in a lawsuit. Here's the first kicker: this is one of the few instances of U.S. jurisprudence when the burden is on the accused to prove innocence.

Here's the second kicker: there's no such thing as an illegal question. There is no interview police in the back room ready to catch you in the act and slap handcuffs on you, and there's no interview jail for those renegades who insist on asking applicants personal questions. But there are questions that may provide the employer with information that could lead to a charge of discrimination.

Let's say that the manager asks the woman wearing the sari (let's call her Indira) where she's from, and she gladly offers that she's from India. As conversations go, after running through questions related to her prior work experience, the friendly manager asks her about her homeland, about Indian food, and about the Indian educational system. The manager ultimately decides to hire another candidate for valid, job-related reasons, and Indira is more than a little upset that she doesn't get the job. She begins to think about her interview and about the focus on her nationality. She begins to believe that perhaps she didn't get the job because of her nationality—even

Yes, you are guilty until you prove your own innocence!

though, in fact, the job went to a more qualified candidate. She goes to the Equal Employment Opportunity Commission (EEOC) and files a charge of discrimination against the employer.

Now it is the company's obligation to prove that it did not discriminate against her when choosing another candidate for this position. Yes, you are guilty until you prove your own innocence!

The additional difficulty is that the jury will attempt to read the manager's mind to ascertain whether he intentionally discriminated against Indira. Asking questions about a candidate's nationality may *imply* unlawful discrimination.

In a court case, Indira's lawyer might ask the manager a series of questions: "Aren't you a busy manager? Don't you value the time you spend during an employment interview? Don't you ask only questions that are important to you in deciding who to hire? Did you, in fact, ask Indira where she was from? Your honor, my case rests."

It's hard to prove that you weren't going to discriminate if you asked these non-job-related questions. And, win or lose, it can prove to be very costly for you to defend the case. For example, it is estimated that the price tag for defending a discrimination lawsuit through a jury verdict is now a whopping $140,000.[5]

Employers found guilty, or who end up settling, often pay much more. In the past 10 years, Home Depot has settled numerous discrimination lawsuits to the tune of $100 million.[6] And that doesn't include the cost of ongoing negative public relations, as people point to your company's experience as an example of the immense expense you incurred in these lawsuits.

It makes a manager want to avoid asking these questions.

> It is estimated that the price tag for defending a discrimination lawsuit through a jury verdict is now a whopping $140,000.

TRUTH

29

It's impolite
(and discriminatory)
to ask about age

Your mother told you that it wasn't polite to ask people how old they are. Not only was she right, but she was also smartly looking out for your professional future (even if she didn't know it). Asking questions about age in the interview can get you slapped—not across the cheek, but across the desk...with a very expensive lawsuit. One individual who didn't get the job based on his age is now suing his prospective employer, Capital University, for $4.6 million.[7] That's a risk you don't want to take.

And the risk is increasing. In 2005, there were 16,585 cases of age discrimination, and of those, the EEOC resolved 14,076 charges in favor of the plaintiffs and recovered $77.7 million in monetary benefits for charging parties and other aggrieved individuals.[8]

It's relatively easy to avoid this costly risk and still get the information you need to make a wise hiring decision.

First, don't ask the obviously dangerous question, "How old are you?" Second, don't even think that you can get around a discrimination charge by getting this information in another way. For example, you can also be found to be discriminatory when you ask the question indirectly, such as "When were you born?" or, "When did you graduate from high school?"

Third, keep your questions focused on performance-related criteria. And ask them consistently of *all* candidates—not just the ones whom you assume can't handle the job because of age issues. You are safe, for instance, if you ask whether the person is at your minimum age requirement ("Are you at least 18 years of age?") when there is a job-related reason to do so.

Or perhaps you're considering a candidate who appears to be elderly and frail. Again, your only concern at this point is whether the candidate can physically handle the job. If you ask *all* your candidates the following question, you can safely ask this candidate the same one: "I've outlined for you here the essential functions of the job. Can you perform these with or without an accommodation?"

> Don't ask the obviously dangerous question, "How old are you?"

The question of age may also pop up when you're considering clearly mature candidates for those positions that traditionally go to recent high school or college grads. The word overqualified naturally comes to your mind. *Overqualified* is a word that can land you in court. The Equal Employment Opportunity Commission (EEOC) has determined that *overqualified* is code for *too old*.

If you're concerned with someone appearing to be overqualified, you might ask, "You seem to have far more experience and qualifications than what is required for this job. Tell me about your motivation for seeking this role."

Be open-minded to the answers you'll receive to that question. The candidate may be recently retired from her main career path but still wants to keep busy in the world. Or the candidate may be starting a whole new career and recognize the value of learning about the industry "from the ground up." The candidate may be reentering the workforce after spending the last decade or so taking care of family, and the entry-level position is a great opportunity to update skills and build relationships in the professional community. Or that person may have financial goals that an entry-level job will help meet, such as saving for an RV or building up her Social Security account.

> *Overqualified* is a word that can land you in court. The Equal Employment Opportunity Commission (EEOC) has determined that *overqualified* is code for *too old*.

TRUTH

30

You wouldn't ask him if he's married—don't ask her either

During the interview, would you ever even consider asking a man about his marital status, the ages of his children, or what his childcare arrangements are? Probably not. The questions are not job related and won't help you determine if this individual is a good fit for the job.

Yet, women are still routinely asked potentially discriminatory questions during the preemployment interview. Questions that would almost never be asked of a male candidate for the same position would be a major tip-off that the question is not legit.

Avoid questions that are typically asked of women and not men.

- Are you married? Single?

- What does your spouse think about...?

- Do you have children? How many?

- What are your childcare arrangements?

- What are your family plans?

- Are you pregnant now?

There are even some astounding reports that some hiring managers are still asking the stupifyingly inappropriate question, "What type of birth control are you using?"

These questions are not job related, so don't go there during the interview. Even the question, "What does your spouse think about your being on the road 50 percent of the time?" is not appropriate, even if it is somewhat job related. Because it's more often asked of a woman, it's off-limits.

It is also wrong to try to indirectly inquire about marital status. One manager was proud of that fact that he had found a way to get a woman talking about her personal life by commenting about any rings she was wearing. Often, this would lead to her sharing information about her marital status. This tactic will hurt you later. If you opened the conversational door and she entered, *you* may have

It is also wrong to try to indirectly inquire about marital status.

to prove later that you didn't use that information when you decided to hire someone else.

If you are concerned about a candidate's ability or willingness to travel or work a set schedule, or about other terms and conditions of employment, ask about *those* issues.

■ This job requires about 50 percent travel, which is a lot. Tell me about any past work experiences in which you had a similar travel schedule and how you managed it.

■ This job involves quite a few weekend and evening hours. Have you worked this kind of schedule before? How did you handle it?

If you are concerned about an applicant's ability to handle childcare responsibilities because attendance and punctuality are extremely important, here are better questions to ask.

■ It is very important for our employees to be at work, on time, every day. Tell me about your attendance and punctuality record.

■ It is important to be at work on time every day. Do you foresee any problems in working the schedule we've outlined?

Again, ask these questions of *all* candidates, not just women.

TRUTH

31

Kind curiosity can kill a career

Generally, we humans are a helpful and caring lot. If we see someone with several bags of groceries, we offer to take one. When we see someone using crutches try to open a heavy door, we offer to help. If we see someone with a cast or someone using a wheelchair, we might ask, "What happened?" But the question, "What happened?" and others like it could get you in a sling during an interview.

If someone appears to be disabled, the same kindly questions you could ask at a party could land you in court if asked in an interview situation. In fact, during the preemployment interview, it is only acceptable to ask, "Are you able to perform the essential functions of this job (that we've reviewed), with or without accommodation?" after reviewing the job description that outlines the essential functions. This question should be asked of all candidates, no matter what their perceived abilities or disabilities may be.

There may be times when someone with a disability will request some accommodation during the actual interview process. This might include an alternative to your written aptitude test (such as being given an oral or untimed test) or inclusion of a sign-interpreter during the interview. As long as the accommodation is reasonable and causes no undue hardship or expense, the law requires you to comply with this request.

If someone reveals a disability, or if it is unclear to you how someone would perform the job given her visible or revealed disability, you can legally ask, "Tell me how you would perform this job with or without accommodation."

Once the candidate has established that she can perform the essential functions of the job, you must consider that individual as a viable candidate. However, only *qualified* candidates—those who can perform the essential job functions—should be considered, and are required to be considered, under the Americans with Disabilities Act (ADA).

> If someone appears to be disabled, the same kindly questions you could ask at a party could land you in court if asked in an interview situation.

Many job accommodations can be made with little expense or adjustment. In fact, 71 percent of accommodations cost $500 or less, with 20 percent of those costing nothing, according to the Job Accommodation Network.

You may also want to demonstrate courtesy to disabled candidates by watching the language you use. For example, you generally wouldn't say that someone is "confined to a wheelchair," but rather, that person "uses a wheelchair." "Persons with disabilities" is greatly preferred over "the handicapped" (which relates back to the old notion of people with disabilities who were often begging with "cap in hand"), or "the disabled."

While offering to help someone with a disability isn't wrong, do so carefully. For example, never take the arm of a visually impaired candidate, but rather, offer your arm for support or guidance. Let the individual guide you on the help and support that is needed and appreciated.

> While offering to help someone with a disability isn't wrong, do so carefully.

TRUTH

32

Avoid questions about religious affiliations

It's been said that you shouldn't discuss religion or politics at a dinner party. While job interviews are certainly no picnic, the same rules apply. Only this time, when the topic is religion, it's a matter of the law.

Federal law dictates that we may not let information about a candidate's faith impact our hiring decision. Therefore, it's up to you to conduct the interviews in such a way that you can't be held liable for discrimination. Most people know better than to ask questions like these.

- Where do you go to church?

- Are you a Methodist?

- Where is your synagogue located?

Another problem area could also be in how you handle the area of scheduling work and interviews. If legitimate business requires that individuals be able to work a flexible schedule, or if your operations schedule regularly involves working on a day of worship, you should ask of *all* candidates: "All of the employees at our shop work regular weekend hours. All employees typically work two Saturdays and two Sundays each month. Is that a problem?"

If candidates indicate that they cannot work on a certain day because of their sincerely held religious beliefs, *don't* simply reject those candidates. Employers are legally obligated to determine if they can reasonably accommodate the candidates, such as by providing a revised schedule. For example, if the schedule generally requires employees to work two Saturdays and two Sundays each month, and the employee can't work on Saturdays because of his beliefs, perhaps he could be scheduled to work on four Sundays.

Similarly, if candidates or employees indicate that they must wear an article of clothing such as a turban or yarmulke required by

> If candidates indicate that they cannot work on a certain day because of their sincerely held religious beliefs, *don't* simply reject those candidates.

their religion during the interview or at work, you have an obligation to allow it as long as it does not impose a burden—an "undue hardship." This accommodation might be as simple as allowing an exception to your dress code policy. However, there may be times that you believe that a robe or other article of clothing may be a safety hazard in your work environment. The difficulty for hiring managers is that there is seldom a time when a one-size-fits-all response works. Managers must often evaluate the facts of any situation and make a decision that balances the needs of the business with the rights of the employee or candidate.

> Managers must often evaluate the facts of any situation and make a decision that balances the needs of the business with the rights of the employee or candidate.

For example, there has been much recent discussion of the rights of Muslim employees in the workplace. Muslims must pray five times a day between dawn and late evening, which means that most employees will be required by their faith to pray two or three times during their workday. While these prayers are brief, workers cannot be interrupted during this time. Usually this can be accommodated during regular breaks, but often a special "floating" break will need to be offered. Some employers offer a special room that can be used by any employee group with prior approval.

Muslim employees also must attend Friday prayer services that take place around midday and last between 45 and 90 minutes.[9] To accommodate this need, you can permit an extended lunch hour.

TRUTH

33

Your mother was wrong; sometimes do be rude

Your mother probably told you to be polite, sit up straight, chew with your mouth closed, and don't interrupt.

Your mother was wrong!

Especially about the part on interrupting. But, then, maybe your mother never had to conduct an interview in today's modern world where discrimination lawsuits are commonplace.

Let's say you begin with a common question like, "Tell me about yourself." It would seem that this is a perfectly acceptable way to get the candidate talking about the things that matter most to her. What happens, though, when you ask a broad question like this—hoping to hear a discussion of past work experiences, educational background, and specific career information—is that you often get a detailed description of the candidate's marital status, number of children, childcare provisions, and a number of other issues that aren't job related. It may be rude, but it won't be wrong: cut her off.

Some managers may naively think that just because the candidate voluntarily shared this information, it is acceptable. What you need to consider is that you are not exempt from a charge of discrimination just because the candidate volunteered personal information.

Since the employer has the burden of proof in any discrimination lawsuit, you, the employer, must prove this information was *not* used in making the employment decision. And if you've hired a man after rejecting a female candidate who revealed issues regarding marital status or children, it may be very hard to prove that the information shared was *not* used in your decision.

Avoid this hazard by sticking to a script of questions that are specifically job related. If you consistently ask the same questions of everyone, it will be easier for you to prove that your interests and concerns were the same for all candidates.

> What you need to consider is that you are not exempt from a charge of discrimination just because the candidate volunteered personal information.

Steer the candidate away from dangerous topics even if shared in a friendly and sociable manner. For example, if you mistakenly ask, "Tell me about yourself" and the candidate suddenly reveals she has 10 children and is divorced, stop the conversation abruptly—even if you feel you're being terribly rude. Your mother may cringe, but she's not there.

> Steer the candidate away from dangerous topics even if shared in a friendly and sociable manner.

Here are some suggestions for ways to shortcut these conversations and steer back to the job-related questions.

- "I'm sorry to cut you off, but I really do want to spend most of our time together talking about the job at hand. So, why don't you tell me more about…"

- "I don't want to be abrupt, but since we only have 30 more minutes for our interview, I want to invest that time hearing more about your work-related experience and education. Let's focus now on…"

- "Let's steer back to the original question, which was…"

- "I want us to focus on the questions I've prepared here in my interview guide, so let me ask you…"

Interrupting may seem awkward or uncomfortable, but it's better than letting the candidate share too much personal or inappropriate information that might be used against you should this candidate not get the job and files a charge of discrimination.

TRUTH

34

Have a vacancy to fill?
You're already too late.

Here's the typical scenario: a top employee in a critical position gives notice. The first thing you do is start the replacement process.

You're already too late. If you've waited until you're officially given notice to start thinking about finding an essential employee's replacement, you've been caught flat-footed. After all, employees casually browse the job market all the time for possible next steps forward or up. (In fact, you probably do, too.) So it's only fair (not to mention strategically vital) that you at least have some ideas— even contacts—ready to deploy when you're given the departing employee's two-week notice.

Just as it takes time to find a new job, hiring managers are also realizing that it takes time to develop relationships, cultivate potential leads, and even groom high-prospect current employees to ensure that top candidates are lined up and ready to roll when a position become vacant.

For one thing, recruiting isn't what it used to be. Consider the college recruiting scene. If you think you can show up on senior interviewing days to get your share of the best candidates, you're wrong. That's too late! Other employers may have been wooing the best students since their freshman year, particularly in cutting-edge fields, like high tech. These forward-thinking hiring managers have been speaking to classes, attending career fairs on campus, advertising in the campus paper, sponsoring collegiate events, developing intern programs, and getting early commitments.

Take a proactive approach by asking your employees to keep an eye on their own replacements. For example, one CEO asks her managers to identify at least three people who could take their place in the case of some catastrophic incident. The team affectionately calls this assignment "preparing

> If you've waited until you're officially given notice to start thinking about finding an essential employee's replacement, you've been caught flat-footed.

to be hit by a bus." Each individual in the organization is asked to think about who could immediately take his place if the worst were to happen. Managers at the firm are encouraged to attend local chamber of commerce and business networking meetings, join professional organizations, and seek out colleagues for lunch, all in the service of having qualified incumbents identified and ready to roll in case the employees should disappear—either suddenly or with notice.

If you ask your employees to cultivate relationships with potential replacements, make sure that they know to say good things about your company when they speak about their jobs. You want good word of mouth as an "employer of choice."

- Accept employment applications and resumes, even when you have no open positions. This allows you to have a ready file of interested candidates.

- Continue to interview candidates, even when there are no vacancies. Look for high-potential employees who might be a good addition to the work team.

- Try to get top candidates onboard even if there's no formal job open. If it's appropriate to their skills and situation, consider giving them short-term consulting assignments or hiring them for part-time work before the vacancy is approved.

- Conduct courtesy interviews with referrals from employees and managers to identify key players.

- Ask each of your reports to identify one to three replacements inside and outside the organization. Brown-bag meetings in which employees give an overview of their jobs and roles will help reveal replacement candidates.

> Encourage employees to recommend their former coworkers, neighbors, and friends.

- Encourage employees to recommend their former coworkers, neighbors, and friends.

- Continually source top candidates by using direct recruitment methods. Often, retailers and other employers needing customer service staff will visit competitors' establishments to identify those providing excellent service and offer a business card or a "talent scout card" encouraging the employee to call.

- Stay active in your field, and attend business networking meetings.

Don't forget your own job. Make sure there's a replacement positioned to take your place, should you have an unfortunate encounter with a bus. At the same time, browse *up* the organization and see which positions you'd like to be groomed to fill.

TRUTH

35

Warning: this resume may contain spin!

As the hiring manager, you have the resume, along with the application form, to give you the information you need in making the employment decision. You have the education information, details on employment experience, and even highlights of the competencies that the candidate brings to the table, captured and summarized in these two forms right at your fingertips.

But is it all accurate? Probably not. Shrewd candidates understand that the resume is their marketing tool and that they can add or delete certain information to make the application form cast them in the best light. You probably did the same thing with your resume.

Candidates aren't necessarily lying, but you can count on the likelihood that they are putting an enormous spin on their background and credentials to make themselves look good. Smart candidates understand the importance of their first impression. The result: you're going to have to do some aggressive digging to get the whole truth behind the applicant's paperwork.

As the hiring manager, you need to have your spin-detector on high so that you can discover the truth about candidates. Here are just a few of the phrases that should make your spin-detector buzz, with possible interpretations:

- *Will discuss* on the application form means that there is a complex story behind the answer you were looking for. And it's probably not a happy one.

- *Open* in the "Salary Requested" or "Last Salary" blanks means there is probably a mismatch in salary—either what you are offering or what the candidate is expecting.

- Blanks on the application form may mean that if the candidate fills it in, it may cost her this job.

> Candidates aren't necessarily lying, but you can count on the likelihood that they are putting an enormous spin on their background and credentials to make themselves look good.

- Omission of dates on the application or resume may mean that some experience or education is outdated.

- Overly vague descriptions may mean that there are damaging details.

- *To be a key candidate making valuable contributions* in the first line of the resume under "Objective" means "I'm using big and formal words to hide the fact that I'm clueless."

- A listing of job duties and responsibilities rather than accomplishments on the resume may mean that the candidate doesn't have achievements that distinguish her from every other applicant.

Once your spin-detector buzzes, ask probing questions that will determine what the candidate may be hiding:

- "You put *will discuss* in this blank. Why? What do you need to discuss with me?"

- "What did you earn at your last job? What are your current salary requirements?"

- "You overlooked this blank on the application form. Could you complete it now?"

- "When did you earn your degree? What did you do in the five years that aren't accounted for on your resume?"

- "Tell me more about what you did in this role."

- "What are you looking for as the next step in your career? What are your motivations for looking for another job?"

- "Tell about two or three of your greatest achievements in your last job."

TRUTH

36

Your candidate may be a scam-didate

The candidate you're interviewing appears to have everything—the right background, perfect experience, and all the credentials you're looking for. But you know what they say about things that appear too good to be true.

And this is about more than just spin. This is about those candidates who go beyond just making themselves look good, to outright lying about their background and credentials.

National scandals have recently focused on the falsification of candidates' credentials on their resumes. Radio Shack's CEO David Edmondson lied on his resume about receiving a psychology degree from Pacific Coast Baptist College in California, where records do not indicate that he even attended at all. Kenneth Lonchar, Veritas Software's chief financial officer and executive vice president, resigned after the company learned he misrepresented his educational credentials, including falsely claiming to hold an MBA from Stanford.[10]

Candidates today commonly "misstate" their background, experience, and credentials. Applicants tend to stretch the truth, with statistics revealing that nearly 36 percent of applications are falsified!

Scam-didates are expensive to employers in many ways. The most obvious expense is the lost time in interviewing, hiring, and on-boarding someone who is destined to fail. Second, there is the expense of precious public esteem that is lost once the employee is discovered. Third, there is the loss of goodwill and respect for management's judgment among the other employees. Fourth, there is the expense of repeating the whole selection process. Finally, your own credibility is cast into doubt.

Fortunately, there are many clues in the application and resume to help you avoid these costly hiring mistakes.

> Applicants tend to stretch the truth, with statistics revealing that nearly 36 percent of applications are falsified!

- **Incomplete application**—If blanks are not filled in or certain information is excluded, it may be that the candidate is hiding something. For example, a candidate who has been fired from a job may conveniently leave the "Reason for Leaving" line incomplete so as not to be automatically disqualified. Some candidates know they would not be considered for the job if you knew they were a poor performer, had a fight with a supervisor, or insulted a customer.

- **Unsigned application**—When the application form is signed, it becomes the formal documentation that the information contained is accurate and that the candidate has truthfully provided the information as to employment history, education, credentials, and skills. If you accept an unsigned application form and then hire the candidate, you may have difficulty terminating her later for falsifying information.

- **Gaps in employment history**—If there are unaccounted periods when the person appeared not to be working or pursuing education, it raises the question about what the individual was doing during those times. Some individuals who want to hide a poor employment experience (in which they were fired or were poor performers) may have gaps in their employment history. Also, individuals who were incarcerated may be trying to hide the fact that they are unable to account for time spent behind bars.

- **Inconsistent information**—People who lie often find it difficult to remember the details of their lies so that they can be consistent when they give falsified dates, names, and places.

- **Erroneous information**—One reason to conduct background checks and make reference calls is to flesh out any untrue information that may be on the application or resume. Were the dates of employment correct? Were the job duties correctly outlined? Can the reasons for termination be verified?

- **Inappropriate reasons for leaving the previous job**—If candidates present an implausible rationale for leaving their employers, they may not be representing their reasons truthfully. The candidate who has been laid off from every job may be stretching the truth.

TRUTH

37

The resume says "yes," but the body language says "no"

The candidate says all the right things. She has all the credentials you're looking for. But you don't feel quite right about her. Another candidate isn't quite so polished, and the credentials aren't exactly right, but you feel like this is the one you should hire. What's going on here?

You may have had a situation where you were talking with someone and you just knew she didn't really mean what she was saying. You may remember a time when you interviewed a candidate and he said he wanted the job, but it didn't seem to register on his face. Or perhaps you can recall a time when you just didn't trust a candidate and later you realized she never made eye contact when talking about her last employer. You could be picking up on nonverbal clues that are not congruent with verbal messages. These are examples of body language not being in agreement with the message that is being expressed verbally.

Everyone expresses himself verbally and nonverbally simultaneously. In an interview setting, when candidates are engaged in the discussion and talk enthusiastically about the position, they tend to exhibit body language that is congruent with their message.

Examples of positive body language include

- The candidate leans his body toward the interviewer. Usually, people face each other when they talk to one another.

- The candidate exhibits good posture.

- The candidate makes appropriate eye contact. This means he neither stares nor is looking down for the majority of the conversation.

- The candidate's arms and upper torso are relatively relaxed. While the job interview setting is certainly a stressful one, and everyone handles that stress in different ways, the candidate's body language shouldn't show embattled defensiveness, such as rigidly crossed arms and legs.

Likewise, negative body language may include the following.

> Everyone expresses himself verbally and nonverbally simultaneously.

- The candidate does not face the interviewer; instead, he is aligned to one side or the other.

- The candidate has slouched posture.

- The candidate may be lying back in the chair or tipping the chair backward.

- The candidate does not make eye contact, or he stares.

- The candidate has crossed arms.

There is a danger in putting too much faith in reading body language.

There is a danger in putting too much faith in reading body language. Some candidates of differing ethnicities or from different countries may have different meanings associated with body language. For example, in many Asian cultures, it is rude to make the kind of eye contact that is generally regarded as appropriate in the United States. Take into consideration differing culture clues to help you interpret body language relatively accurately. There are also times when the room is cold, so the candidate has his arms crossed during the interview to keep warm. It could also be that the candidate has a physical limitation—or even nervous knots in his stomach—making good posture difficult or uncomfortable.

In any case, carefully consider the clues by asking yourself if this behavior is indicative of a cultural issue, if it is consistent throughout the interview or just at certain times, and what other verbal signals are being expressed. Don't overlook total meaning, derived from intonation and voice inflexion.

TRUTH

38

The receptionist test—
better than salt?

There's a hiring story that's been around for some time about an IBM executive getting ready to make an offer to a job candidate. But first he took him out to lunch. When the candidate salted his food before tasting it, the executive ruled him out and offered the job to another candidate instead. What was it about the salt? According to the executive's reasoning, the fact that the candidate didn't fully analyze his food before salting it revealed that he probably wouldn't fully analyze a high-stakes business situation before taking action. An urban legend? Perhaps, but it points to the efforts that some take to get a quick behavioral understanding of a potential hire.

Over recent decades, the emergence of behavioral psychology theories and refined interviewing techniques have led to hiring managers looking for ways of seeing into a candidate's soul by the simple, unconscious choices the candidate makes during unguarded moments. Does the candidate salt the food first? Reach for the pepper first? Part her hair on the right or left?

Here's a simple personality test that will reveal volumes about the candidate's ability to fit into your company's culture: How does the candidate treat the support staff while in your office for the interview?

Your support staff is the first gate your candidates must pass through when going through the interview process in your company. And that staff is in a perfect position to report behaviors—positive or negative—observed while applicants are waiting for their interview. This isn't a matter of choosing between coffee or water when staff offers refreshments while the candidate waits. It's an issue of whether the candidate says "please" and "thank you."

For example, consider the candidate who was condescending to the receptionist when he reported for the interview. And then when he had to wait longer than he felt he should have had to, he barked orders to her. He was loud

Here's a simple personality test that will reveal volumes about the candidate's ability to fit into your company's culture: How does the candidate treat the support staff while in your office?

and rude and never once apologized for his behavior. This particular organization valued team spirit. Its choice about this particular candidate was an easy one.

There was also the time that a candidate did not complete his application. He brought a friend to complete the application since he could neither read nor write. Because the job in question required excellent written and verbal communication skills, the hiring manager once again decided to pass on the candidate because of the receptionist's being in a perfect position to spot what was going on in the waiting area.

The way the candidate behaves with you and your entire team can tell you all you need to know about that person's ability to fit into your company culture.

- If you take the candidate out to lunch, how does she deal with the host or wait staff? Is she professional and respectful, or does she make demands in a rude and unprofessional way?

- Does the candidate take personal cell phone calls during your interview time together? There are countless stories about candidates taking personal calls on their cells during an interview, never to apologize or explain about the urgency of receiving a call. (Yes, there are times that it would be acceptable, for example, if the candidate's parent or spouse were just whisked from emergency surgery into recovery.)

- If recruiting for sales professionals, does the candidate continue to sell herself to you and your assistant in a professional and appropriate manner, especially in light of your sales team's style?

- How does the candidate interact with other colleagues in casual contexts, such as lunch or evening receptions? Is she relaxed yet professional? Is she guzzling martinis?

Keep in mind that your candidates are also going to be conducting behavior tests of their own. Are *you* polite and respectful to your receptionist? Do you keep your appointments on time? Do *you* hold your calls during interviews? And, if you pepper your Cheerios, you might want to keep that to yourself.

39

Don't send away candidates dressed for a day at the beach

It wasn't too long ago when there was no mystery to dressing for an interview. No matter what kind of job they were applying for—from stockroom clerk to administrative assistant to pizza deliverer to sales rep—candidates would come in dressed in some version of executive wear, complete with suit and tie. But now, even executives are coming to work in polo shirts and chinos, so it's impossible to say what "dress for success" means anymore. One founder of a start-up actually chose the candidate for a sales position who rolled into his meeting direct from a camping trip in the Colorado Rockies (complete with the smell of smoke from the campfire) over the slick, spruced-up applicant who arrived equipped with suit and tie. The camper had the spontaneous passion she was looking for, while Mr. Put Together was suspiciously *too* slick. And, in Silicon Valley, where team interviews are generally part of the selection process, it's not uncommon for candidates to be rejected by their would-have-been colleagues because they overdressed for the interview. They were seen to be out-of-touch with the organization's culture—not to mention the overall fashions of the high-tech world.

The applicant who has just brushed the sand off her sandaled feet and left her surfboard drying in your parking lot may, in fact, be more motivated than the applicant who spent a leisurely morning dressing just so for the job interview. The question for you is whether that person is a match for the job, your company's culture, and your expectations. If so, it's up to you to help the candidate improve her chances of success by overlooking the style gaffe and going to the heart of her personal drive.

As you schedule the interview with candidates, let them know what kind of dress is appropriate for the meeting. If your company is sincerely business casual, don't make them scrounge around in the back of their VW for a crumpled tie they remember having thrown there in the distant past. If, however, your office environment is indeed more

> The question for you is whether that person is a match for the job, your company's culture, and your expectations.

formal, letting them know in advance that ties (ironed ones at that) are expected will help them decide whether your company's culture is right for them and whether they want to go through the extra effort every morning of actually putting on socks. This will save you both precious time.

Complete a thorough interview and determine if the candidate has the qualifications to do the job, regardless of his appearance at the moment. If you're looking for creative genius who won't have customer interaction, it won't really matter what that person looks like. (Nobody really cared if Einstein had a haircut, right?) If, however, your position is for a food server and the candidate shows up with dirty fingernails, appearance is an important clue to the person's natural aptitude for the job.

Cut the youngsters a break. Even if your workplace is formal, entry-level employees typically don't have grown-up business clothes. And if they do, they probably will look supremely uncomfortable in them. Accept that awkwardness as a passing phase that they'll quickly grow out of. Be willing to kindly and gently coach young employees on your dress code and what is appropriate in your workplace.

> Kindly and gently coach young employees on your dress code and what is appropriate in your workplace.

Model the kind of business dress that is appropriate for your workplace. If you expect your employees to dress and behave with a certain level of sophistication and dignity, do so yourself.

Obviously, there are times when you would expect a candidate to be dressed appropriately without prompting—when interviewing for mid- and top-level roles, when reviewing candidates with past professional work experience, and for highly selective roles for fresh MBAs. However, when dealing with young candidates just out of high school or technical school, you may want to see if they are, in fact, diamonds in the rough. Shoes can come later.

40

You aren't an elephant

You're only interviewing a few people. The job has very straightforward requirements. If the candidate meets those requirements, you'll know within five minutes of the interview. So, you think, surely you don't need to take notes. You'll remember the highlights of each person. After all, you'll have the application form in front of you. That will jar your memory, if need be.

If you don't think you need to take notes during the interview, think again. It may be easy to remember exactly what a candidate has said if he was the only candidate interviewed. But when you are interviewing multiple candidates for an open position, or worse yet, multiple candidates for multiple open positions, it becomes far more challenging. Even if you were interviewing only one candidate for one position, thorough note-taking could mean the difference between a successful hire and epic regret.

Don't rely on your memory alone when making one of the most important decisions regarding the future of your organization. It's so easy to take notes that will allow you to recall important details, document your decision, and help defend your organization if there is a charge of discrimination.

- **Tell the candidate what you're doing**—Inform the candidate early in the interview you'll be taking notes. Let the candidate know why you're taking notes by saying, "I'm going to be taking notes during our conversation together. This will help me record the important information you'll be sharing and will help us select the best person for the job."

- **Don't write on the application**—Remember that the application form is a legal document and that it should only contain the handwriting of the applicant. Therefore, take notes on an interview guide, if you've developed one for use with all candidates, or on a separate sheet of paper.

> Even if you were interviewing only one candidate for one position, thorough note-taking could mean the difference between a successful hire and epic regret.

- **Write down key words and phrases**—There is no need to write down every word. If you do this, you won't be fully listening to the candidate.

> Keep a steady pace of note-taking through the good and the bad.

- **Don't write down just the negative information**— If candidates see you jump into action with your pen every time they say something that they know they might regret later, they'll start editing their answers, comments, and stories. Keep a steady pace of note-taking through the good and the bad.

- **Note any red flags in your notes**—Even though you'll be steadily taking notes through the good and bad parts of the interview, circle issues you'll want to ask additional questions about.

- **As you're interviewing the candidate, circle any items to probe further or come back to later**—If you feel you haven't heard a complete answer or that something is questionable about the candidate's response, make a note so you can go back to this issue and ask more probing questions.

- **If you've identified ideal or benchmark responses prior to the interview, make notes of how the candidate's responses align with the benchmarked responses**—Make notes about the issues that support the benchmark alignment. (In other words, document why you have rated this candidate's responses as positive, negative, or neutral.)

- **Avoid any codes that might be misconstrued as discriminatory**—Never mark the candidate's gender, race, ethnicity, religious preferences, family situation, or other discriminatory issues in your notes. These notes may end up documenting the fact that you *did* discriminate when making your hiring decision.

- **Remember that this is documentation of your employment decision**—Use language supporting your employment decision and ensure that no discriminatory comments are made.

TRUTH

41

Keep on selling to candidates

Consider this scenario.

A hospital, known regionally as an Employer of Choice, had no difficulty in getting qualified applicants for open positions. But when the hospital made offers, it had few takers. An outside consultant conducted focus groups and asked managers the question, "Why should I work for you?" "Why should any good candidate work for your organization?" This bright group of managers didn't know how to answer these questions; they assumed that any bright candidate would understand that their hospital was an Employer of Choice.

The problem wasn't that these managers were unconvinced of the many good benefits and working conditions the hospital offered. They just didn't know they needed to actively sell today's candidates on the benefits of working with their organization.

These managers needed to talk about what their organization offered. They needed to stress their competitive salary and top-notch benefits. They needed to talk about their commitment to work-life balance. They needed to talk about their values and how patient care was their number-one priority. They needed, in fact, to sell the hospital to the candidates. Otherwise, perfectly good candidates slipped away, leaving perfectly good positions unfilled.

Valuable candidates—whether they are active seekers or passive browsers—might have been attracted to your organization because of a direct contact, a telephone call, or a direct mail campaign. They might have been initially interested in your organization because of your compelling recruitment message or the charisma of the individual who contacted them. But you have to *keep* them interested and engaged throughout the entire selection process; otherwise, they might disappear on you.

In a difficult labor market, you must continue to sell candidates through the time that the offer is made and accepted:

- Analyze and identify your strengths in selling to prospective employees.

> You have to *keep* them interested and engaged throughout the entire selection process.

- Use a "cheat sheet" of the talking points of why your company is a great place to work. You might consider creating a one-page summary of these benefits for candidates to take home with them so that they can weigh the benefits of your organization against other opportunities.

- Listen for hints from the candidates about what is important to them and respond to these issues by talking about what you have to offer. For example, if a candidate continues to comment on the lack of advancement with the current employer, be sure to talk about all the things your organization does to help employees advance.

- Consider giving candidates the opportunity to talk with current employees about what it's like to work at your company. Being given the chance to say good things about their organization has the added benefit of giving employees the chance to remind *themselves* of what a good employer your company is. So not only will you be hiring a new employee, but you might also be keeping a current one who had forgotten how good it is at your company.

If you want a great candidate relationship, treat that person as you would treat a customer. The Disney organization, for example, has long understood the importance of providing excellent service to its internal and external customers. So, in addition to hiring mystery shoppers to evaluate the quality, service, and cleanliness of its facilities, it has used mystery shoppers to evaluate the job search experience of its applicants.

> If you want a great candidate relationship, treat that person as you would treat a customer.

Since using mystery applicants is not practical for most hiring managers, some managers have developed candidate comment cards or look for ways to touch base with candidates to gain their appraisal of the process. A final strategy to help you improve your own empathy toward job seekers is to go on job interviews yourself. Many hiring managers forget about how intimidating the process can be, how vulnerable you feel as an applicant, and how stupid some of those interview questions can be. By playing the role of "constant candidate" and going on interviews now and then, you can help improve your selection process.

TRUTH

42

Invest in telephone
screening to save time later

In a tight labor market, it's tempting to try to interview anybody with any promise. Shouldn't you cast your net far and wide to create a better pool of candidates? Especially when the employment history, educational background, and credentials look right on target on the application and resume, don't you want to get that qualified candidate in your door as soon as possible?

Slow down.

You may find yourself interviewing applicants who don't have the basic necessities for the job, like the applicant for the mechanic's position who doesn't have a driver's license. Or you may have an applicant who seems perfect for your vacancy but who expects a salary double that of what you can offer. And there may be that person who seems to have outstanding credentials as an outside sales person but is unwilling to meet the travel requirements for the job.

While you don't want to let good candidates slip away, and you might be able to talk some candidates into changing their minds about travel and compensation, some candidates will never be a good fit with the position. And if you have to do too much convincing at the outset, you can be sure that that candidate will be a high-maintenance employee once the job begins.

Further, your time is valuable (as is the candidate's), and you certainly don't want to waste your time scheduling the interview and investing in an hour-long interview only to discover that the candidate is totally wrong for the job.

Ideally, you want to maximize the effectiveness of your time when you're responsible for hiring the best candidates. One strategy is to use prescreening interviews on the phone before the face-to-face interview to determine if that investment of time is worthwhile for both of you.

By conducting prescreening interviews, you'll be better able to ensure that each candidate has the

> Ideally, you want to maximize the effectiveness of your time when you're responsible for hiring the best candidates.

basic qualifications, skills, abilities, and interests needed for the job; check the compensation expectations of the candidates to determine if they are within range; and underscore key issues and questions on which to focus in the face-to-face interview. Best of all, you can eliminate candidates who are not a good fit with the job.

Predetermine "knock-out" factors

The first step in using a prescreening tool is to first determine what constitutes "knock-out" factors—factors that immediately determine if the candidate is right for the job.

- Ability to work a set schedule or a variety of hours

- Possession of basic skill sets

- Availability for weekend or evening work

- Possession of a credential or license

- Openness to travel if required by the job

- Possession of specific job-related skills, such as proficiency in a foreign language, welding, or data entry

- Minimal educational background

- Specific job-related experience

- Ability to perform the essential job functions (for example, lifting, standing, giving instructions)

- Compensation expectations

Job requirements should always be job related and specific for the available position.

Schedule appropriate candidates for the next selection step

Determine, in advance, what kind of responses are acceptable or unacceptable. For example, is it necessary to be fluent in Spanish or is proficiency acceptable? What would proficient mean in the context of the work requirements? How similar must the candidate's past job description be to the current position? Can the candidate perform the essential functions of the job, with accommodation?

Once you've determined what constitutes an "A" candidate, take the time necessary to conduct this initial screening process on the phone before inviting the candidate to come to your workplace for a face-to-face interview. You'll find that your list of appointments may be shorter than it would have been otherwise. But, in this case, you'll be very glad to have the quality instead of the quantity.

TRUTH

43

Face-to-face doesn't have to be in-person

You have identified three outstanding candidates that you'd like to schedule for interviews. Unfortunately, your staffing budget is small, and the travel costs for flying these three candidates to the interview carries a hefty price tag, especially since you want them all scheduled yesterday. But you have no choice if you want to conduct anything beyond the telephone interview, which you've already conducted.

Don't overlook one of the least expensive and easiest alternatives to the in-person interview given the advent of video conferencing technology: the video interview.

Many employers are turning to video interviewing to avoid travel and related costs. Especially since 9/11, video interviewing has been adopted as a solid recruitment strategy. Third-party recruiters are using video interviewing as part of their solution to reach candidates for their clients—their employers. Even universities and community colleges are offering video options for campus recruitment efforts.

In addition to the obvious monetary advantages related to sparing expensive air travel and hotels, video interviewing offers additional, unique advantages. For example, all the hiring decision makers can view the resulting videos. And current technology and sources for video interviews make this approach easy and convenient for both the interviewers and the interviewees.

Video interviews are relatively easy to set up. You use the same set of questions that you would use in your face-to-face interview. In the case of a taped interview, you submit these questions in advance. Interviews can be conducted almost anywhere, making it easier for candidates who live in rural areas or for companies based in hard-to-reach locales. The college employment office, the third-party recruiter's office, or even the candidate's home may be possible interview locations.

Of course, video conferences are not without drawbacks. When using taped video interviews, the hiring team that wasn't present for the actual interview won't have a chance to ask probing

Many employers are turning to video interviewing to avoid travel and related costs.

questions for clarity or additional information. From the candidates' perspective, some get nervous in front of a camera and may have trouble feeling that they've achieved the necessary rapport with their interviewers. From both perspectives, everyone's expectation for the "Q" factor—that certain something that professional television personalities radiate on camera to project warmth, charm, and professionalism—is inflated simply by their everyday exposure to professional television. Anything less than superb polish and outgoing, bright friendliness will feel disappointing and flat. Not everyone, in other words, has either the face or personality for television. And that would be an unnecessary liability for both sides of the interview.

> Interviews can be conducted almost anywhere, making it easier for candidates who live in rural areas, or for companies based in hard-to-reach locales.

In the case of taped interviews, candidates don't have the chance to ask questions and assess the desirability of the job opportunity from their point of view. While the disadvantage to the candidates is obvious, this one-sided conversation also poses a disadvantage to the hiring manager. Employers can tell a lot about candidates from the questions they ask—how they think, what their priorities are, and so on.

Of course, one of the biggest potential liabilities is that the videotaped interview is now fully documented, which means that hiring managers need to be on their best behaviors to avoid discrimination lawsuits.[11]

44

Too many cooks might improve the broth

You've heard it a million times before: too many cooks spoil the broth. And you know firsthand what a nuisance it can be to have a teeming multitude of people personally invested in a project. It often becomes unwieldy, chaotic, and impossible to make a decision. You've seen it time and time again in your many meetings, committees, and task forces. Too many people mean too little work, too much talk, and not nearly enough action.

So, you think, I'm going to make this employee selection decision on my own. I can make the decision more quickly; we can have the whole process behind us, with our new employee on board in no time.

But will this unilateral decision be a better decision? Maybe not.

There may be times when you should have your entire team involved in selecting the best employee. If you have self-directed work teams, or if team involvement is critical to your culture and the trust you've developed in your work processes, you will want to involve key members of your team. Or perhaps this position is one that interacts with many different departments or levels; it may be best to have all those interfacing with this position to have some input into the final decision.

Sometimes a group decision will give you the feedback and confidence you need to make the best employment decision. So you need to determine the most effective and streamlined processes to get the group behind this critical decision.

Recently, a credit union needed to replace its retiring CEO, and the board of directors wanted to be involved in the process. As a team, the board and an external consultant decided on the candidate criteria and developed questions for the interview guide.

> If you have self-directed work teams, or if team involvement is critical to your culture and the trust you've developed in your work processes, you will want to involve key members of your team.

Since the selection team would be together for each interview, the members decided that place-name markers would be helpful for the candidates. The consultant posed questions to each of the candidates from the guide, and each board member asked follow-up and probing questions if needed. The consultant facilitated the candidate evaluations. It was a successful process that allowed each board member to have a voice and offer input to this major decision, permitting the organization to select a top CEO.

Two strategies for involving critical constituencies include panel interviews and multiple interviews. In panel interviews, all of the interviewers are present at one time for one interview; multiple interviews involve one-on-one interviewing with more than one interviewer. For either panel or multiple interviews, you need to consider who is on your selection team:

- The hiring manager

- A coworker

- Someone who has unique knowledge or expertise who can better assess the competence of the applicant

- The hiring manager's supervisor or other interfacing managers

Begin by training all employees involved in the process on effective interviewing skills, including how to avoid discriminatory questions. Inform all team players as to protocol issues such as who will ask questions and how probing questions will be handled.

> The point is to get appropriate participation, yet not have a candidate leave feeling beat up by the process.

Let the candidate know what to expect and about the role the employees will take in the hiring decision. Make sure that the candidate is introduced to each member of the team and understands the role of each person.

In panel interviews, one person often asks all the questions. Then the employees at the interview can actively listen to the responses and make notes of probing questions to ask. If employees will be asking these follow-up questions, inform the candidate in advance. The point is to get appropriate participation, yet not have a candidate leave feeling beat up by the process.

After the interview, ask each interviewer to carefully assess the candidate in the areas of educational background, work history, "knock-out" areas, and core and job competencies. This permits each person to provide a take on the candidate and note any concerns or problem areas. Ideally, the interview team should meet and review one another's evaluations to agree on the individual who is the best fit for the position.

TRUTH

45

Make haste slowly

An insurance company's financial manager tells the story of a resume that he received that was right on the money. This resume contained all the qualifications required by the job, and then some. After talking with the candidate by phone, the manager became even more certain that this was the candidate who should be hired, and now—before he got away. The manager had been searching for a candidate who possessed just these qualifications for months, and he knew that someone with these attributes wouldn't be on the market for long.

But the company had a policy of doing a complete background check—a time-consuming step that frustrated the hiring manager. "We're going to lose this candidate," he complained. "And it's all going to be because of this inane, bureaucratic policy!"

The human resources manager won the argument, which turned out to be a good thing. The background check revealed that the resume had been sent from prison, where the highly qualified candidate was finishing up his sentence for embezzlement. He was clever with finances, all right.

Any industrial psychologist will tell you that the best predictor of future performance is past performance. And, since you rarely learn all about candidates' past performance from the resume or in the interview, an even better way of discerning past performance and verifying credentials is through background and reference checks.

Background checks may be time-consuming, but by following a step-by-step process, you'll have the necessary information to make an informed decision.

1. **Get permission from the candidate in advance—** Most employers have an application form with a statement requesting that information regarding past employment be released by previous employers and institutions verifying credentials.

> Any industrial psychologist will tell you that the best predictor of future performance is past performance.

2. **Get the contact information from the candidate**—Let the candidate know you won't make an employment decision until you have received favorable references and verifiable information. Ask candidates about who to call and how you might best be able to reach the individuals noted.

3. **Don't call the human resources department**—Most HR departments have strong policies about not providing reference information to potential employers, with the exception of verifying basic employment information. It's better to call the former supervisor, who can speak to the performance of the employee.

4. **Let the individual know that the candidate gave you permission to call**—Begin by saying, "Hello Mr. Supervisor! Joe Worker has given me your name as someone who would be willing to provide information on his work history with your company. We are considering Joe for a position in sales, and I'd like to ask just a few questions. Is now a good time to talk?"

5. **Verify factual information first**—There is the least amount of resistance to answering fact-based questions in the reference-checking interview. Verify name, title, and relationship of the individual being called, company name, job title and duties, dates of employment, reason for termination, and salary history.

6. **Ask about the positive and negative attributes of the candidate**—There is typically little resistance to questions about positive attributes, unless the individual has been a terrible employee. Asking about negative attributes will receive the most resistance. The reason is that many employers understand they have a potential liability for libel or slander if they share negative, unsubstantiated information. Therefore, couch these questions diplomatically, and only after you've verified the factual information and learned the strengths.

7. **Ask questions that may help you better manage the new employee**—No one knows better than past supervisors about the management style that was most effective in dealing with the candidate. Ask specific questions to

help you determine the unique issues in dealing with this individual, such as "What advice could you share with me in managing this individual?"

8. **Wrap up with some key questions**—While there are no truly "magical" questions in conducting reference checks, be sure to ask, "Is this individual eligible for rehire?" and, "Is there anything else I need to know?"

TRUTH

46

You may want to hire candidates even when they get a bad reference

You want to check on references because you know you'll get information on the past behaviors of candidates. While it's easy to assume that a candidate with a bad reference predicts a track record of poor performance—and, therefore, you should pass that person up—that particular candidate could be just want you need. And want.

Carolyn, a training manager candidate, had everything going for her. She was bright, enthusiastic, and possessed all the right credentials. She seemed perfect. So naturally, the hiring manager's next step was to check her references. But Carolyn had a slight smudge on her record, so she said, "I don't think you're going to get a good recommendation from my last supervisor."

"Why's that, Carolyn?"

"Well, he was a difficult manager. In fact, if I were to characterize him, he was mean-spirited and even verbally abusive at times. We had differing viewpoints on many issues, and I challenged his approach since I didn't believe it was in the best interests of the organization."

With that as background, the hiring manager made the call. Carolyn was right. Her previous manager had nothing good to say about her. He told the hiring manager that Carolyn was combative, that she was difficult to work with, and that he could not recommend her. This was definitely a very bad reference.

However, Carolyn was being kind when she characterized him as mean-spirited. During the interview, he was rude, sarcastic, and borderline abusive with the hiring manager.

The hiring manager thought about the decision for some time and finally decided to hire Carolyn. It was an excellent decision. Never once did the manager experience the combative and difficult-to-work-with behaviors that her former supervisor observed.

> While it's easy to assume that a bad reference predicts a track record of poor performance... that particular candidate could be just want you need.

Not all people see reality in the same way, and sometimes you have to trust your gut to determine who has the best grasp on reality, and therefore, who the best candidate really is. When you encounter conflicting perceptions regarding the candidates you interview, especially during the reference checking process, take these actions.

> Not all people see reality in the same way, and sometimes you have to trust your gut to determine who has the best grasp on reality.

- Let the candidate know you'll be checking references. Get any insights on what the reference will say prior to your call by first checking with the candidate. Tell candidates, "I'm going to be calling your past supervisor. What am I likely to hear?"

- Listen to what the candidate says about references. Get an idea about what you might expect, and prepare your questions accordingly when calling the reference. Keep in mind that the candidate has likely read books and articles about job-hunting, all advising him to say only good things about previous employers. So the candidate may be struggling to frame past experiences in as positive a way as possible. If you otherwise like the candidate, try to gently elicit some additional details about the past work experience, so you can get a fuller—and more accurate—picture of what really happened with the previous employer.

- Don't expect the past supervisor to be as unpleasant or uncooperative to you as he was reported to have been to the employee. People can usually be on their best behavior to strangers, especially to people they perceive as being their equals.

- Call another reference or two if possible, even personal references. See which story is the different one.

Often, as a manager, you must make judgment calls, and this is one of them.

TRUTH

47

Beware the "Whizzinator"

Drug testing has become a standard step in the hiring process. Employees have become accustomed to the potential indignity of this essential aspect to finding a job. Employers are routinely making the successful passing of a drug test a condition of employment. With such rigorous and scientific screening procedures in place, one would think that drug users couldn't find a job anywhere. But, as every employer knows, workplaces are still vulnerable to users and addicts. They manage to outsmart the system.

> Employers are routinely making the successful passing of a drug test a condition of employment.

Recently, the Committee on Oversight and Investigations on Capitol Hill investigated the use of a device known as the "Whizzinator," a prosthetic "urine delivery system" designed specifically to beat preemployment drug tests.[12] "Helping workers cheat on drug tests is a big business," stated Diane Cadrain in *HR Magazine*. She also reported that a Google search using the term "beat a drug test" gets more than a million hits, and "pass a drug test" gets more than three million.

And advice is used by drug test dodgers, with varying results. One hiring manager reported a call received from the testing lab after it processed a sample from a candidate. The caller said, "I have good news and bad news. The good news is that your candidate passed the drug screen. The bad news: he's pregnant." Apparently, the candidate had brought in his wife's urine for the test. And apparently he was in for a good news/bad news joke of his own that day.

Another hiring manager tells the story of receiving another call from a lab, saying that this time the urine was not even human. Think about this long enough, and you start to wonder how the applicant got the sample.

A drug-free workplace isn't an ideal that's entirely out of reach. You just need to be extra vigilant in your procedures.

- **Use a professional service that specializes in drug screening**—Most drug-testing services offer several options for testing—on-site specimen collection by the lab, collection at the drug testing company's location, or tests that are administered by the employer and then sent to the lab for verification and further testing. These testing companies have policies and procedures in place to foil the Whizzinator.

> A drug-free workplace isn't an ideal that's entirely out of reach. You just need to be extra vigilant in your procedures.

- **Consider the timing of drug tests**—Although employers may administer drug tests prior to employment offers, many who also conduct post-offer medical exams combine these two tests to save money and time. Medical exams may not be required before an offer of employment is extended.

You'd think that just telling candidates your policy is to test for drugs would scare away those who take drugs, wouldn't you? But then again, they are on drugs!

TRUTH

48

Be real, even if scary

The last thing you want is to scare good candidates away, right? You've worked hard to develop powerful recruitment messages. You've created strategies to reach out to wish-list candidates. You've invested a lot of time and money in your recruitment efforts, so you want to make sure you put your best foot forward.

But you're beginning to see a trend. One day into the new job, or maybe it takes as long as a week or a month, your precious new hire quits. The trend has developed into a pattern, so you must give up the word *coincidence* as an excuse. It's time to do something drastic.

Just as it's possible to oversell a job opportunity, it's also possible to underemphasize some of the more, well, *real* aspects of the job that may ultimately send a sadder-but-wiser new employee packing. You might as well come clean sooner than later. It will be harder to recruit candidates at the outset, but a new hire who quits within hours or weeks of her start date is worse than no hire at all.

The solution: give the candidates an opportunity to get a real, complete picture of not only the job but also all that comes with it. Maybe it's a scheduled round of really bad hours. Maybe it's a population of clients who are unpleasant, even violent. Maybe it's simply a dingy workplace environment.

Employers who have observed high turnover and realize that their jobs may not be for everyone are putting into practice the realistic job preview (RJP)—giving their employees the chance to really see what they're about to get themselves into.

For example, one agency that served people with developmental disabilities realized that not all people felt called to this work. It found that by offering a view of their facility and clients, it could screen out unlikely candidates early in the process and devote its attention to more promising applicants.

You can use RJPs at any stage of the employment process. Some organizations, such as a manufacturer needing second-shift workers, need to advertise bad

The solution: give the candidates an opportunity to get a real, complete picture of not only the job but also all that comes with it.

news boldly in their recruitment advertising. Or the RJP can be part of the initial onsite screening process. For example, one employer—losing so many employees because it found its sterile work environment so distasteful—decided a tour of the facility should be one of the first steps in the selection process. This was also preceded by a detailed description during the telephone screening interview so candidates could self-select out of the process if they believed they would not enjoy this environment. Another employer—a customer call center—decided after interviewing that it would provide a job tour and invite top candidates to listen in on employees dealing with customers by phone.

When the realistic preview is offered depends on these issues:

- Cost of different elements of the interviewing process

- Number of people who are unlikely to find this work or work environment appealing

- Logistical elements

- Retention rates and retention thresholds

You can also use RJPs as enticements! The leaders of one hospital believed they had such an impressive work environment that if nurses could just experience it for even a short time, they could attract these nurses. The organization advertised that if nurses would invest one morning or afternoon checking out the work opportunities through tours, talks with nurses, and a preview of the hospital, they would receive a check for $50. Many nurses came and applied out of curiosity. When they discovered what a wonderful environment this hospital offered, many of these nurses decided to join the hospital staff—just as the management had predicted.

You can also use RJPs as enticements!

49

No crystal ball?
Try employment testing.

With so much emphasis placed on interviews, it's easy to forget that the interview alone is a fairly inaccurate means of discerning the candidate's skills, abilities, and competencies. As interviewers, we tend to be swayed by first impressions. We get distracted by our own desires to make a good impression ourselves, especially if we're hiring for a hard-to-fill position or we have a highly desirable candidate in front of us. We fail to ask the probing questions that reveal the rest of the story.

How can you *really* know that this is the right candidate for the job? You need a tool to help you see beyond the interview. That tool is the preemployment test.

You may use a number of different types of tests to select candidates for the job. Those tests include work sample tests or virtual job tryouts, personality profiles or work style inventories, integrity tests, and aptitude tests.

The simplest and most straightforward tests are *work sample tests* and *virtual job tryouts*—those that test some specific skill required in the job. If you want a welder, you'll use a test that assesses the candidate's ability to weld. If you want an administrative assistant, you'll test for typing accuracy, as well as knowledge of the various spreadsheet and word processing software packages. These tests may include a real work sample or one similar to those experienced on the job.

Personality tests may include such tests as the Myers-Briggs, the 16PF, or the DISC. They test personality traits such as extroversion/introversion, dominance/passivity, and openness to change. While these tests are growing in popularity as a preemployment tool, there is also controversy surrounding the use of these instruments. Most of these tests weren't designed to be preemployment tools, so critics say that their results are misused in a hiring context.

For example, the Myers-Briggs is a common assessment tool typically used for personal and

> You need a tool to help you see beyond the interview. That tool is the pre-employment test.

team development. But it was never designed as a preemployment tool, and its use in preemployment selection has been challenged. Other tests, such as the Minnesota Multiphasic Personality Inventory (MMPI)—also one never designed as a preemployment test—have been challenged in the courts for invasion of privacy since many personal questions are asked.

> You should only use tests that have been independently validated.

Integrity tests, or paper-and-pencil honesty tests, are often used by organizations employing large numbers of entry-level and low-wage workers or blue-collar workers. Integrity tests try to determine if the individual is likely to engage in questionable activities. They may ask questions about punctuality, attendance, work ethic, honesty, illegal drug use, alcohol abuse, and criminal activity.

Aptitude tests determine an individual's potential for certain skills and abilities, including mathematics, verbal skills, space visualization, and mechanical reasoning.

Here are some important considerations to keep in mind when deciding whether to use a test as part of your preemployment screening process.

- **Is the test valid?** You should only use tests that have been independently validated. Validity studies try to determine, through mathematical calculation, if a high score on the test correlates with strong job performance. Simply put: validity studies test the test.

- **How reliable is the test?** Do you know that it consistently measures what it is supposed to measure?

- **What is the cost of the test?** Is it costly to administer? (Does it take up too much time for the hiring manager or the HR professional?) Does the test provide a return on investment? (Does the improved quality of the hiring decision provide more value than the cost of the test?)

- **What are the timing issues?** How long does it take to administer the test? How long is the turnaround time in receiving results? Will this slow down the hiring process? When will the test be administered?

■ **What are the administrative issues to be considered?**
Where will the test be administered? Is there a private
or quiet area for individuals to take the test? If the
test is timed, who will time it? Is equipment readily
accessible for any work sample tests?

50

Graphology: palm reading or valid tool?

You want to know what the candidate is *really* thinking and how this candidate will perform in your organization. You can ask great interview questions, but these questions may or may not reveal the truth about that candidate.

What would be ideal, you think, is if you could get inside the head of your candidate and figure out what's really going on. Then, you think, you can make a better, more informed decision. Maybe you could just hire a palm reader to figure out the whole truth. Or maybe you could use graphology—the practice of analyzing handwriting.

That's exactly what 85 percent of European companies do in their selection process. And it's not just considered hocus-pocus anymore in the United States. Over 3,000 organizations, such as GE, Ford, and the Central Intelligence Agency, use graphology in their preemployment procedures. And the use of graphology in the United States for preemployment purposes is on the rise.

Graphology requires a one-page sample of handwriting, usually a short essay written by the candidate on unlined paper. Expert analysts look at the loops, the slant, the unusual letters, the pressure used, and the dots on i's—all to get a picture of the personality and temperament of the individual.

Employers like using graphology because it's relatively inexpensive, easy to administer, and perhaps one of the most objective personality assessment methods since candidates don't know how their "answers"—their handwriting—will impact their results.[13] Hiring managers also benefit from an analysis of some of the key indicators of job success and performance, including traits such as honesty and integrity and critical issues such as motivation.

> Employers like using graphology because it's relatively inexpensive, easy to administer, and perhaps one of the most objective personality assessment methods.

There is still quite a bit of controversy surrounding handwriting analysis as a preemployment tool since it is not a foolproof method of picking top performers. But many employers argue that the results are as reliable as those obtained by personality tests.

While there are schools in Argentina and Italy that offer accredited degrees in handwriting analysis, graphologists in the United States receive their training through correspondence courses and seminars. There is no certification that is universally recognized within the field. Therefore, hiring managers should use caution in selecting a graphologist and check references from other employers who have used this individual or organization for preemployment testing.

Balance the use of graphology with other selection tools, such as interviews, background and reference checks, and job preview

It's also wise to balance the use of graphology with other selection tools, such as interviews, background and reference checks, and job preview so that your decision isn't based on graphology alone. Be sure to evaluate the success of this tool to determine yourself if it's palm reading or a valid and reliable selection tool.

51

The last one you interview only seems like the winner

You've just interviewed 20 candidates for your open position. You feel like you have a good pool of highly qualified candidates. As you think back on all the candidates, you are especially drawn to the last candidate you interviewed. Very strong credentials. Great answers. Seemed enthusiastic. You believe you know who the winner is.

But not so fast!

The truth is, if you try to "wing it" in evaluating candidates, the tendency is to favor the last candidates interviewed. In psychology, this is called the *recency effect*, in which there is a cognitive bias toward the most recent stimuli or observations. If you interview 10 candidates, you are more likely to remember the strengths of the last candidates interviewed, creating a bias toward these candidates. Therefore, you need an objective way to capture your observations and rate each candidate as you go along so that you don't fall victim to the recency effect and other forms of interviewer bias.

One way to accomplish this goal is to develop an evaluation form in which all candidates are rated on the same scale and then reviewed to determine the best fit for the job. By creating an evaluation form, you can eliminate the recency effect from the selection process. Since you will have completed your evaluation immediately after each interview, you can give each candidate the same objective review. And, as a side benefit, you can maintain documentation for the rationale behind the employment decision, which may help provide the support needed for employers to defend a discrimination lawsuit.

To create a solid evaluation process that keeps all candidates equally eligible until you make the final selection, determine in advance what skills, abilities, and knowledge are necessary for this role and what value each attribute should be assigned. You can do this by assessing the skills, abilities, and knowledge of your most successful incumbents as compared to

In psychology, this is called the *recency effect*, in which there is a cognitive bias toward the most recent stimuli or observations.

those possessed by your average employees. Next, create positive and negative benchmarks for each attribute evaluated and include these benchmarks on an evaluation form.

When conducting a panel interview or multiple interviews, have each interviewer complete a separate evaluation form for each candidate interviewed. This permits each interviewer to independently assess each candidate's strengths and weaknesses and highlight any concerns without regard to the comments and suggestions of other interviewers. When conducting multiple interviews, meet with all the interviewers to compare evaluation forms. Focus discussion on areas of disagreement and try to discern why the discrepancies exist. Try to reach consensus on the ratings for each candidate.

As you go through the interview process, frequently review—and rereview—all your notes from the previous interviews. This not only keeps your memory fresh, but it is also a mental trick to keep all the candidates appearing equally current in your mind. And, now that you know about the recency effect, should Candidate 7 still appear to be a better choice than Candidate 3, you can double-check with yourself to make sure that the recency effect isn't coloring your preference.

(Since you'll be keeping evaluations as a tool to document your employment decision, be sure to eliminate any comments that are either not job related or are potentially discriminatory. These include comments such as marital status, age, children, religious affiliation, ethnicity, race, and gender. Always avoid codes that might be construed as potentially discriminatory, such as "SWM" for "single, white male," as they could serve as documentation that the company was focusing on discriminatory criteria.)

> When conducting a panel interview or multiple interviews, have each interviewer complete a separate evaluation form for each candidate interviewed.

TRUTH

52

The one who offers salary information first is the loser

When it comes to the employment transaction, for generations the power of choice has been with the employer. As a result, even if we know better intellectually, it's easy to operate on the unconscious assumption that we have the luxury of a broad selection of eager applicants while the candidate we finally choose is waiting for just one opportunity from just one likely employer (namely us). So it often comes as a surprise to discover that after we spend the necessary time carefully deliberating among a boiled-down group of, say, three or four possible hires, our final selection has options of his own!

Ensuring that the offers you make will actually be accepted by today's sophisticated—and often passive—job seekers is a daunting task. You're competing with unknown employers out there who may be outbidding your salary offer and snatching up the best candidates. But you can increase your chances of success when developing candidate offers.

- **Always determine, as early in the process as possible, how much the candidate is making and what his salary expectations are**—In fact, the one who reveals a desired range first is often the loser in salary negotiations, since the one with the information is in a more powerful bargaining position. If you ask the question first about the candidate's expectations, this puts you at an advantage when making an offer. For example, if you know that the candidate has been making far less than your beginning range, chances are good this individual will not be put off with a salary toward the low end. However, if the candidate has been making far more than your range, you may need to think about ways you can make your offer more appealing.

- **Determine what the candidate is currently receiving in terms of benefits and working conditions**—Perhaps the candidate is working second shift, and you are offering a first-shift job—the candidate's

> Ensuring that the offers you make will actually be accepted by today's sophisticated—and often passive—job seekers is a daunting task.

preference. Or think about ways you can show the candidate how your benefits package is better than the candidate's current package, or what competing companies are offering.

- **When talking to the candidate, try to compare apples to apples**—If you offer a lower base salary but are offering benefits that more than make up for less money, be sure to talk about this advantage. Stress the total compensation package—base pay, incentive pay, and direct and indirect compensation.

- **Discuss the intangible benefits of working with your organization**—Perhaps you offer a unique working environment, or your company has a culture that emphasizes advancement from within, coupled with ongoing training and tuition advance assistance. Talk about the other positive features your company has to offer: company reputation, stability, outstanding products and services, safety record, industry leader.

- **Let the candidate tell you**—Ask the candidate what it will take to make the offer irresistible. You may be surprised. It could be intangible benefits or a simple request that you can easily accommodate. Even the mere fact that you asked could put you at an advantage over other companies who might make the candidate a take-it-or-leave-it offer.

- **Close the sale**—Once you've made the offer, roll out the welcome mat! Let your candidate know how personally excited you are at the prospect of him coming to work at your company; how everyone has been waiting for someone *just like him* to fill that desperately needed position. Show him that you see him as more than just an acceptable resume; you see him as a *person*—the perfect fit, with just the right set of abilities and just the personality to fit right in.

- **Provide time for a considered response**—Some candidates may want to think about your offer, look carefully at the numbers, and discuss the offer with family members or friends. Offer a reasonable time for the candidate to accept or reject the offer. Be flexible as well with your timing. If the candidate needs to take a two-week vacation between jobs (or if he's getting married six months into his new job), *you* be the one to accommodate that need for flexible time. Your competition down the street might not.

TRUTH

53

Don't tell candidates why they weren't selected

Have you ever experienced a situation in which you received calls from pesky candidates, begging you for information about why they didn't get the job? You start out trying to be nice—after all, you've read the advice in job hunting books that, as a candidate, you should ask "why" when you aren't selected for a job. But, after a while as the one doing the hiring, after three or four of these conversations, you feel as though the life is being sucked out of you. Depending on your own personal endurance, it doesn't take too long before you are tempted to make your answer short—cruelly short: "We just didn't like you," or "You have no personality," or "You have last week's garlic on your breath."

One hiring manager tells the story of one such applicant, who begged and begged the manager to share some information so she could learn from her mistakes and do better for the next interview. After some thinking (and several calls from her), the manager thought, "What could be the harm in telling her a few things?" There's plenty of harm. She immediately wanted to debate the manager on his conclusions, challenge his thinking, and ultimately, she demanded that he change his mind.

You have no legal responsibility to share with candidates the reasons they weren't selected, except to say, "We selected someone who was a better fit with our organization's needs." This is the precise phrase you should use. Not, "We selected the best candidate for the job," because "best" may be construed as having the most education, the highest credential, or the most work experience. These criteria may not, ultimately, make for the best fit of a candidate.

For example, let's look at two candidates for an outside sales role. The position requires selling heavy

> You have no legal responsibility to share with candidates the reasons they weren't selected, except to say, "We selected someone who was a better fit with our organization's needs."

industrial equipment, calling on manufacturers and other industrial clients. Candidate A may have the "best" qualifications: 10 years in outside sales in promoting office supplies, a bachelor's degree in business management, and stellar evaluations from prior employers. However, the candidate who is best suited for the job, Candidate B, may have fewer years of experience and only some college; but she also has outstanding references, 9 years in selling a competitive line, calling on the same customers your company wants to target. In this case, Candidate A may be "best," yet you know that Candidate B is better suited. Further, you may find that Candidate B has excellent verbal communications skills, is highly articulate, and has excellent persuasive skills, while Candidate A has only average skill levels in these important areas.

> When internal candidates are competing for promotional opportunities, provide feedback to each internal candidate to identify opportunities for professional growth and development.

There are several exceptions to this rule of feedback, however. When internal candidates are competing for promotional opportunities, provide feedback to each internal candidate to identify opportunities for professional growth and development, to create an action plan for coaching on areas in need of improvement, and to improve morale by providing this individual with an opportunity to qualify for the next open position in the organization.

You might want to take the time to share information with *external* candidates when there is a solid reason as to why they were not selected and you want to cultivate a relationship with them in case there's an opening that's perfect for them in the future. Some of these objective criteria include the following:

■ Lack of credentials essential for this position (for example, a captain's license for a boat captain role).

- Inability to meet the work schedule or conditions of employment (For example, the candidate cannot work weekends or evenings, is not willing to travel as required by the job, or doesn't want to work in a manufacturing environment.)

- Inadequate years of experience as required for the job. (Be certain all candidates must meet this hurdle before offering this as your rationale.)

- Lack of diploma, degree, or technical achievement essential to this job.

- Salary expectations beyond the range for the open position.

References

Truth 5

1   Information on job-hoppers from "Are Job Hoppers the Smartest People in the Workforce?" by Jeff Westover, *College Recruiter*, accessed in http://www.collegerecruiter.com/.

Truth 6

2   Manager reports on benefits from refugees from Andrea C. Poe, "Refugees to the Rescue," *HR Magazine*, November 2000.

3   Number of refugees obtained from Jeanne Batalova, PhD, "Spotlight on Refugees and Asylees in the United States," Migration Policy Institute, August 1, 2006.

Truth 20

4   Information on Container Stores from "Finding Workers Who Fit," Vicki Powers, *Business 2.0*, November 2004.

Truth 28

5   Costs of defending an employment case from "Texas: Cutting the cost of employment litigation," by *Business and Legal Reports, Inc.*, April 2006.

6   Discrimination lawsuit costs from "Discrimination Lawsuits Cost Home Depot Millions," May 31, 2006, *Personal Injury Lawyers*.

Truth 29

7   Sources for charges of EEOC age discrimination cases found in http://www.eeoc.gov/types/age.html.

8   Sources for recent age discrimination litigation found in Kathy Lynn Gray, "Capital University sued for $4.6 million," *The Columbus Dispatch*, September 27, 2006, accessed in http://www.columbusdispatch.com/news-story.php?story=d ispatch/2006/09/27/20060927-B3-01.html.

Truth 32

9   Information regarding Muslim employee accommodation is from "Showing Good Faith Toward Muslim Employees," Marc Adams, *SHRM On-line*, Winter 2001.

Truth 36

10   Information on the Veritas scandal from "Veritas CFO Resigns Over Falsified Resume," 10/03/2002, from http://www.thestreet.com/markets/marketfeatures/10045724.html.

Truth 43

11   Mike Frost, "Video Interviewing: Not Yet Ready for Prime-Time," *HR Magazine*, August 2001.

Truth 47

12   Information on workforce drug testing from *Critical Components of Workplace Drug Testing*, SHRM White Paper, Kara Blumberg, SPHR, July 2004.

Truth 50

13   "The Write Stuff: What the Evidence Says About Using Handwriting Analysis in Hiring" by Steven L. Thomas, Steve Vaught; *SAM Advanced Management Journal*, Vol. 66, 2001.

Acknowledgments

As with any book, there are many people to thank. I owe many thanks to Jennifer Simon, acquisitions editor at Pearson Education, who diligently worked with me to configure my knowledge and experience into the "Truth About" format; and to Russ Hall for his insights and support in this endeavor. A huge thanks goes to my good buddy and professional colleague, Martha Finney, for her authorship skills and knowledge of HR—and most of all, for her belief in me. Mike Losey, the former CEO of SHRM, was also instrumental in bringing this project to my attention. Thanks Mike! I also want to thank my wonderful clients and seminar participants who have over the past 20 years provided me with great stories and examples that were used in this book. I don't know what I would do without the help and support of such friends as Elizabeth Jeffries, Ed Cherof, and my SHRM and NSA buddies. And I must also thank the Society for Human Resource Management for its role in my professional development throughout my career. Finally, a big thank you goes to my husband, Jim, for his love and support.

About the Author

Catherine D. Fyock, CSP, SPHR, is an Employment Strategist and Principal of Innovative Management Concepts in Crestwood, KY, providing insights on recruiting and retaining the best employees in an aging and changing workplace. She frequently helps organizations develop strategies to reduce turnover and improve productivity through their human resource management. She provides innovative learning events and consulting services for managers and HR professionals on employment-related issues. The author of five books, she frequently writes for professional journals and industry publications, and has been quoted in the *Wall Street Journal*, *USA Today*, *Money*, and *Worth*. She can be reached at cathy@cathyfyock.com and through her web site at http://cathyfyock.com.